I0467590

Tattoo Your Skin With Animals

How To Tattoo Animals On Your Skin

Animal Tattoo

By : Gala Publication

Published By :

Gala Publication
© Copyright 2015 – Gala Publication

ISBN-13: **978-1522706984**
ISBN-10: **1522706984**

Table of Contents

Learn To Draw Animal Tattoo 10 Characters:.......
Learn To Draw Bear Tattoo.....................................
Learn To Draw Bird Tattoo ....
Learn To Draw Bull Tattoo.....................................
Learn To Draw Bulldog Tattoo ....
Learn To Draw Cat Tattoo......................................
Learn To Draw Koi Tattoo......................................
Learn To Draw Native American Tattoo.................
Learn To Draw Spider Tattoo ....
Learn To Draw Tiger Tattoo...................................
Learn To Draw Werewolf Tattoo............................

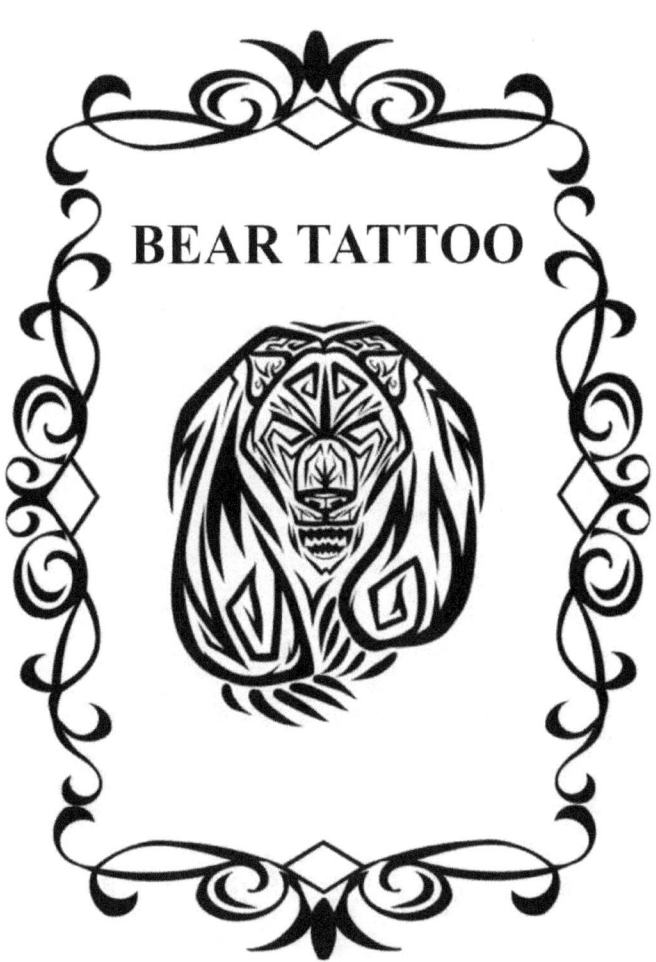

BEAR TATTOO

STEP 1

STEP 2

STEP 3

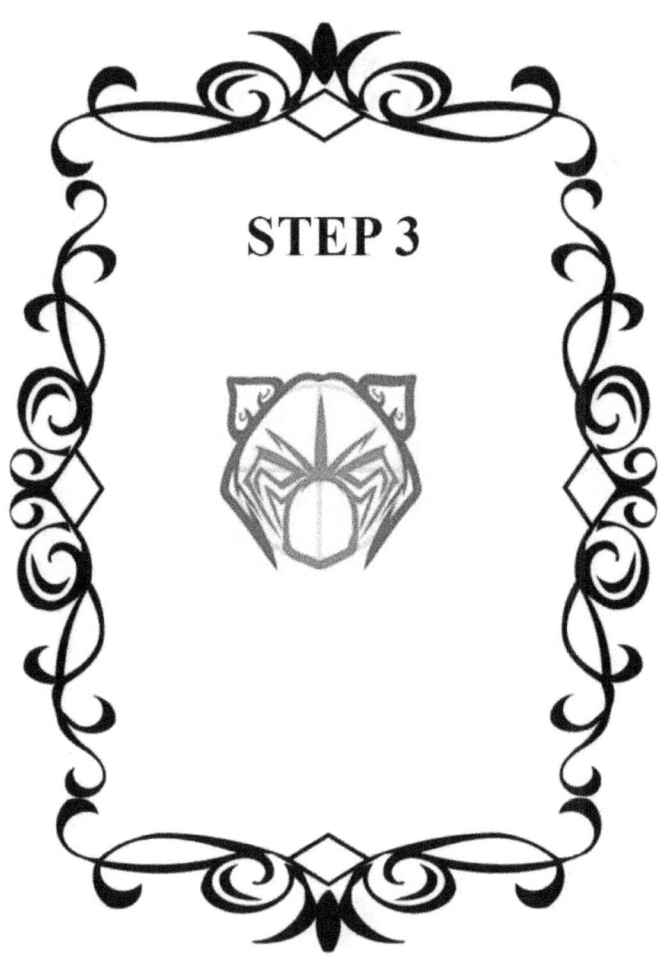

STEP 4

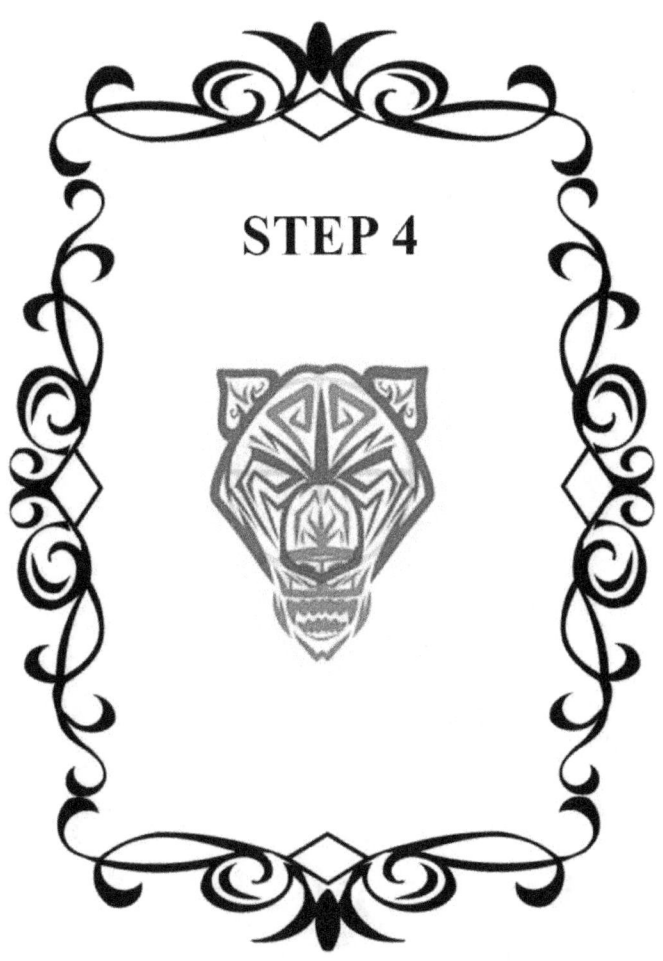

STEP 5

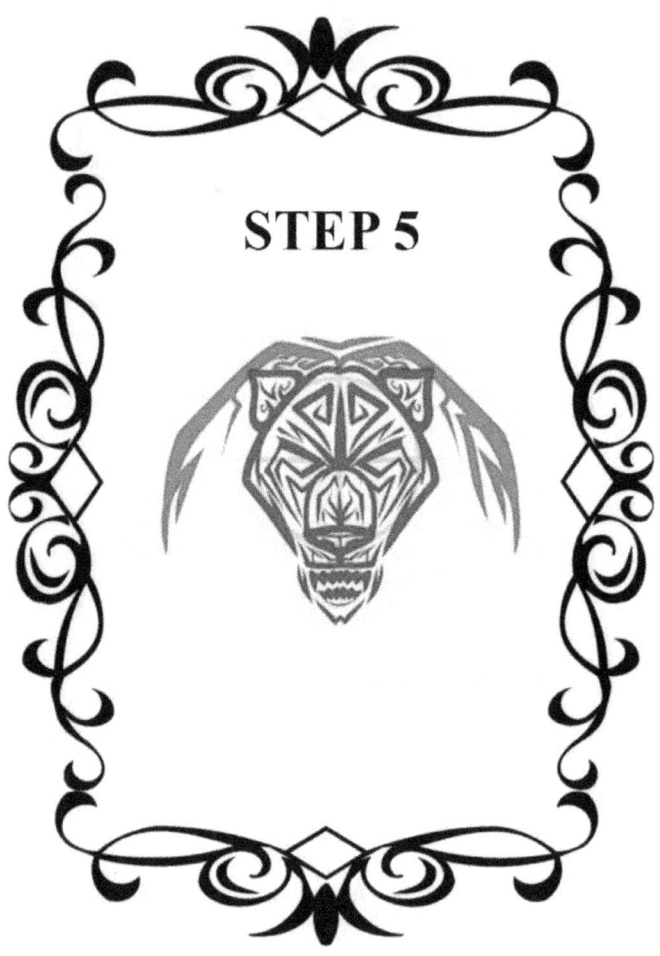

STEP 6

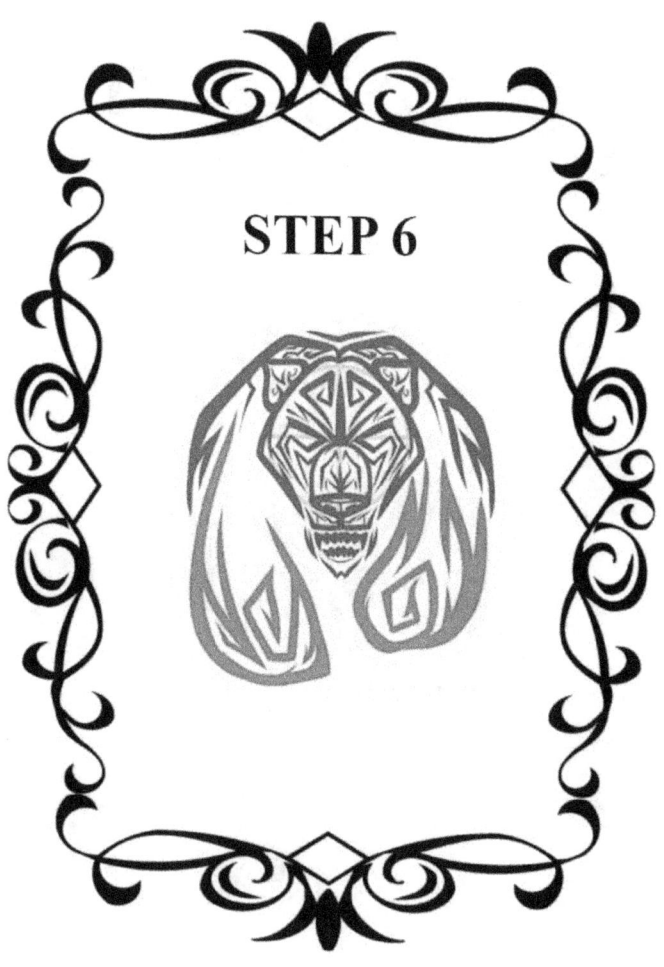

STEP 7

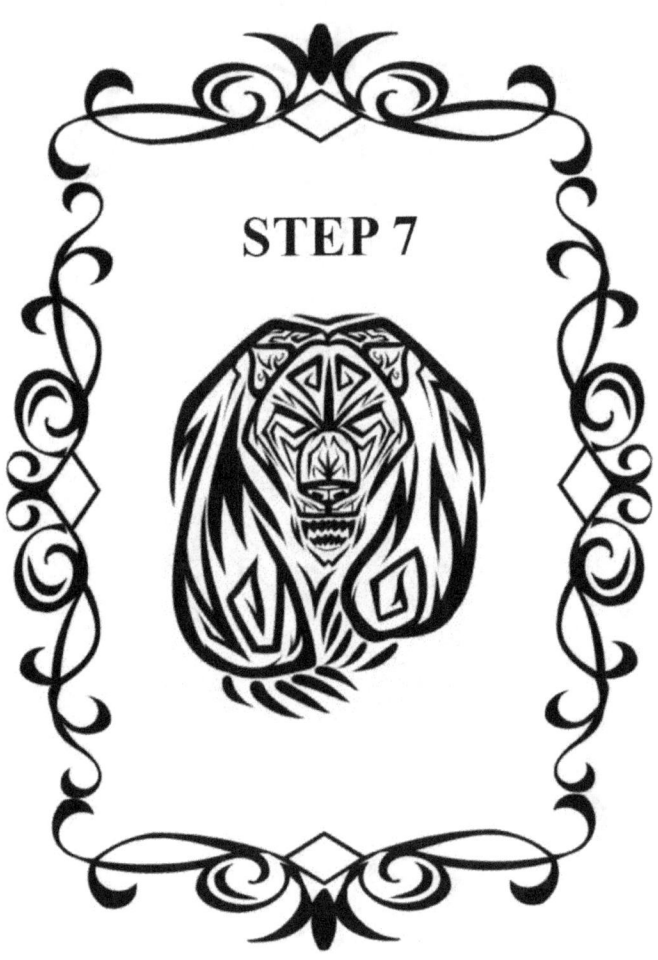

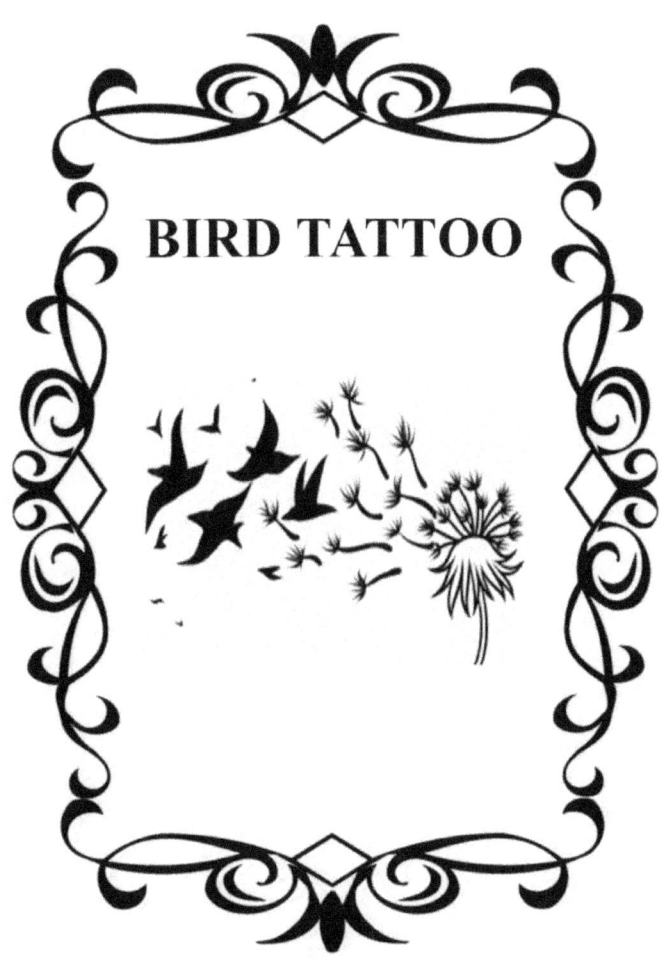

BIRD TATTOO

14

STEP 1

STEP 2

STEP 3

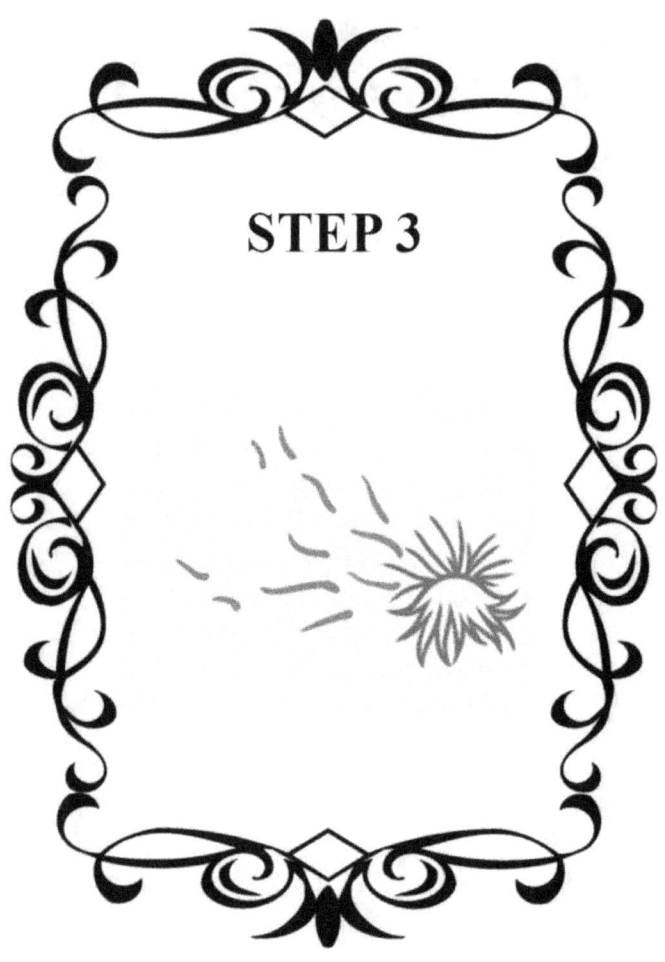

STEP 4

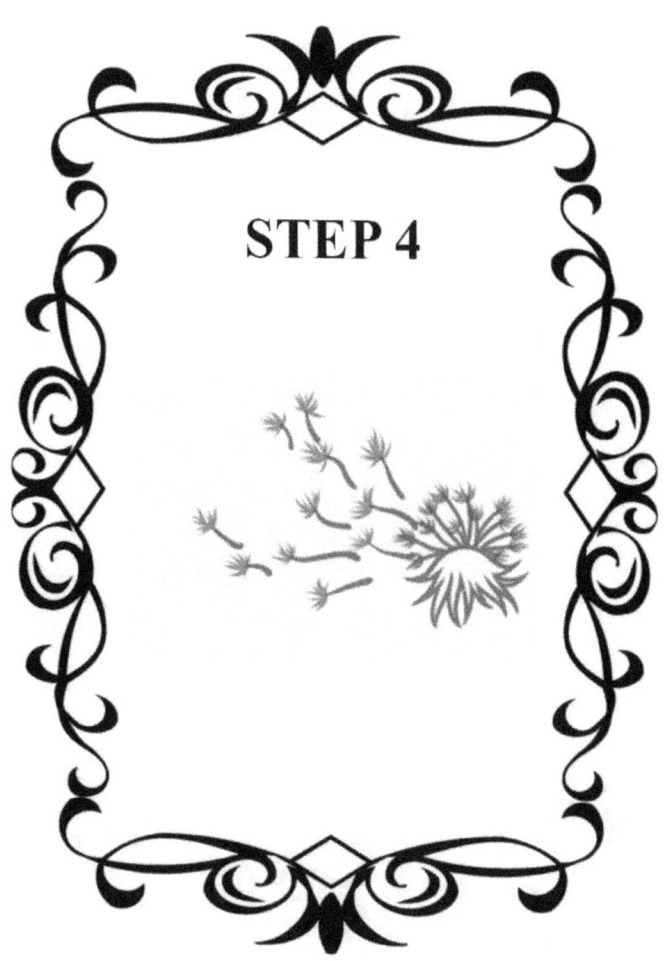

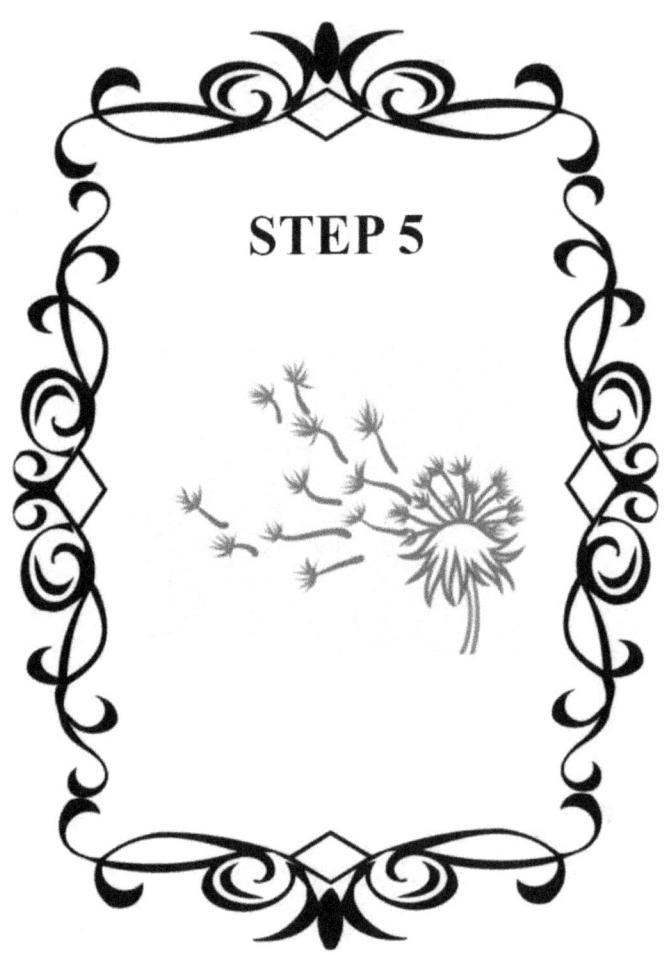

STEP 5

STEP 6

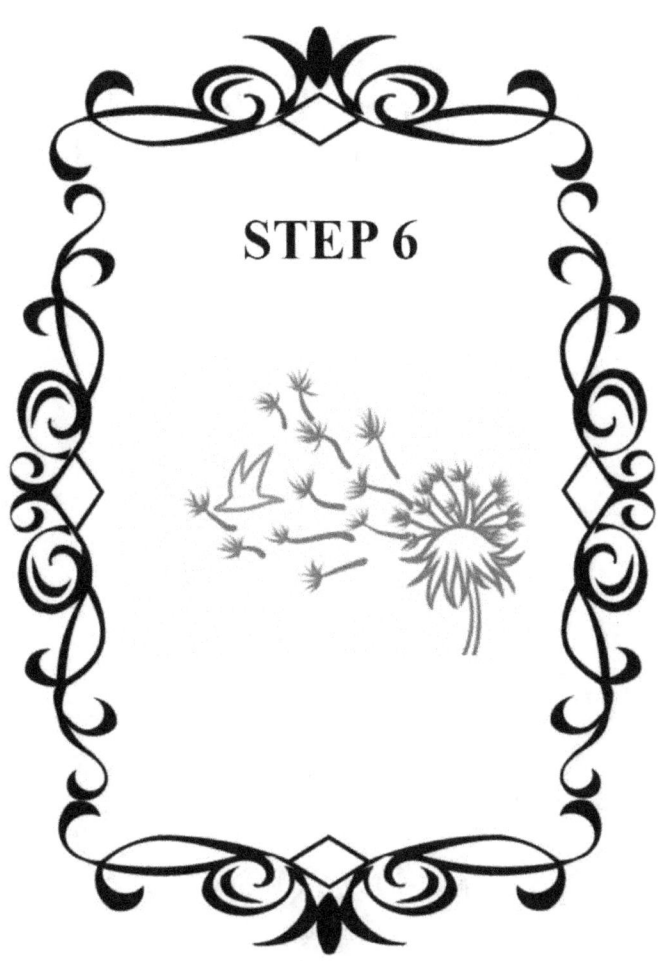

STEP 7

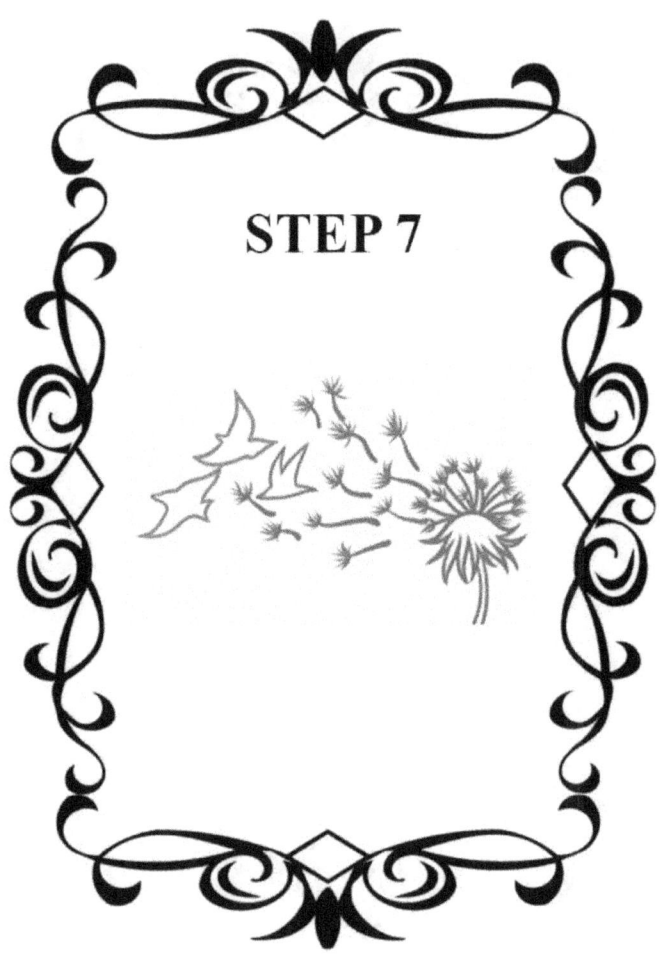

STEP 8

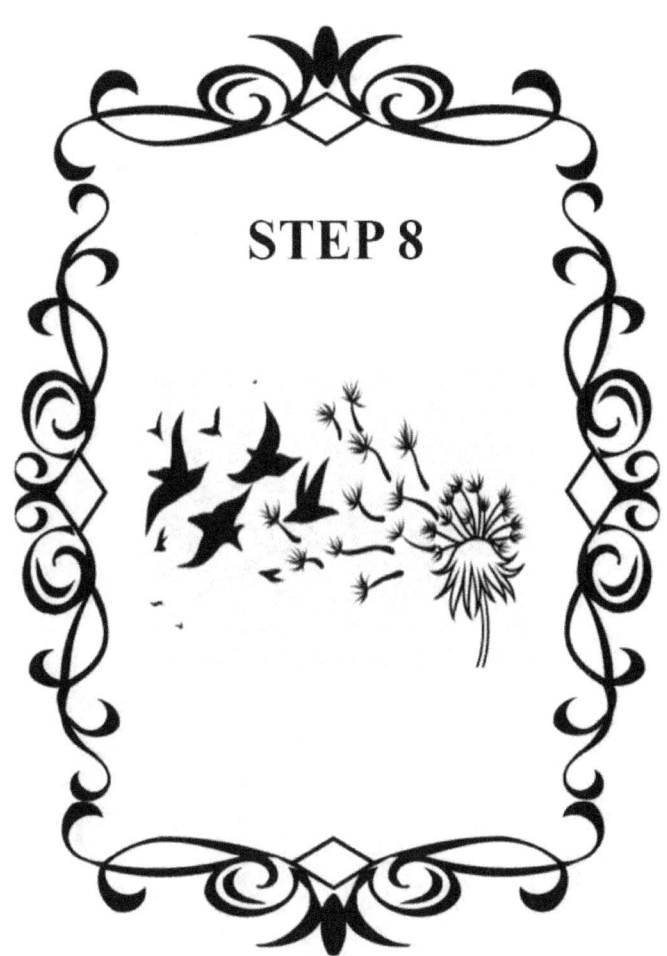

BULL TATTOO

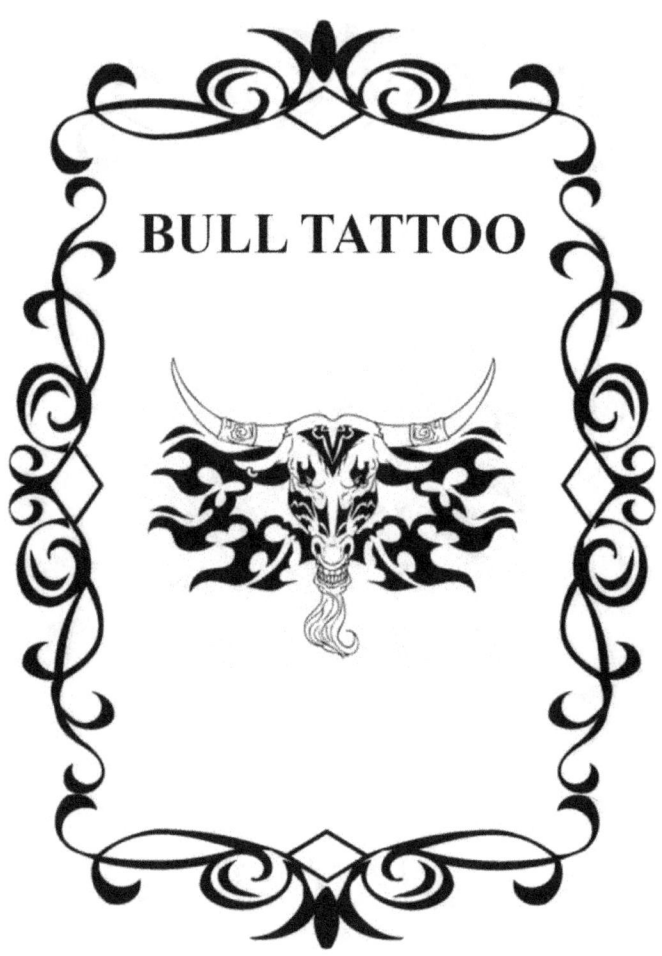

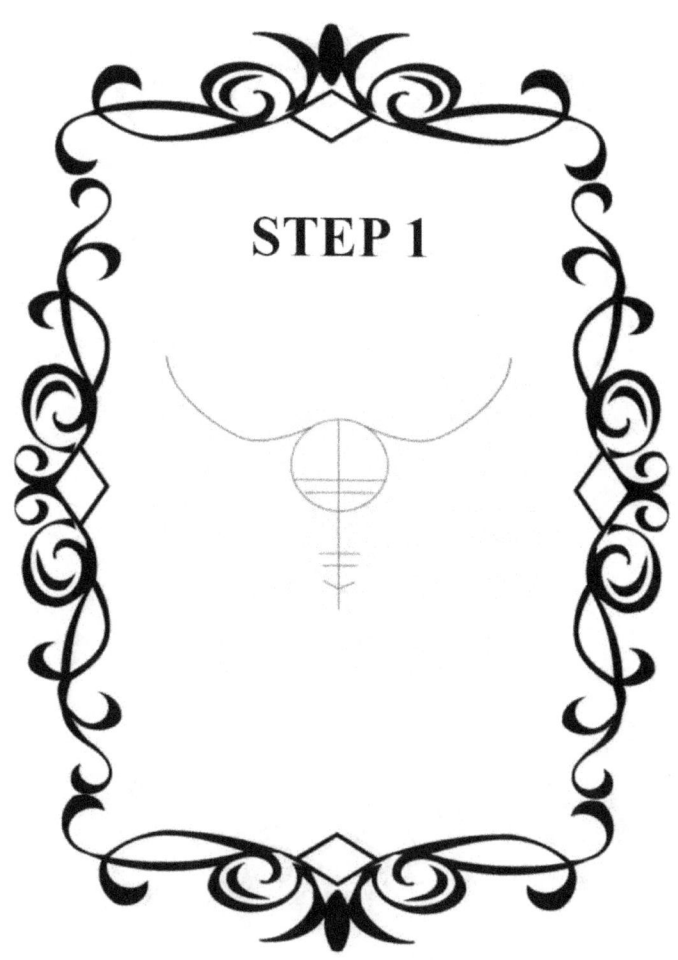

STEP 1

STEP 2

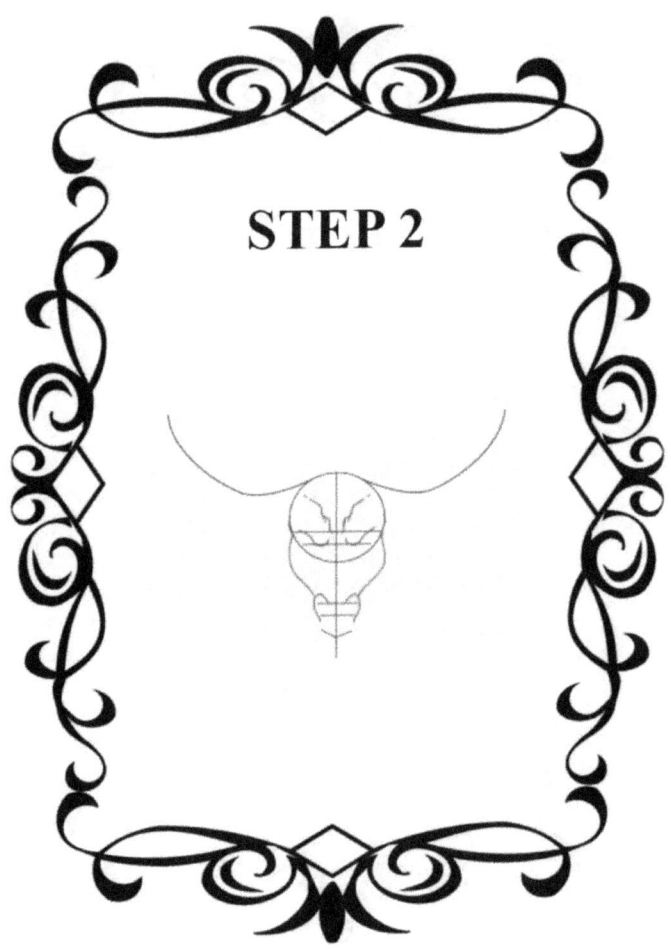

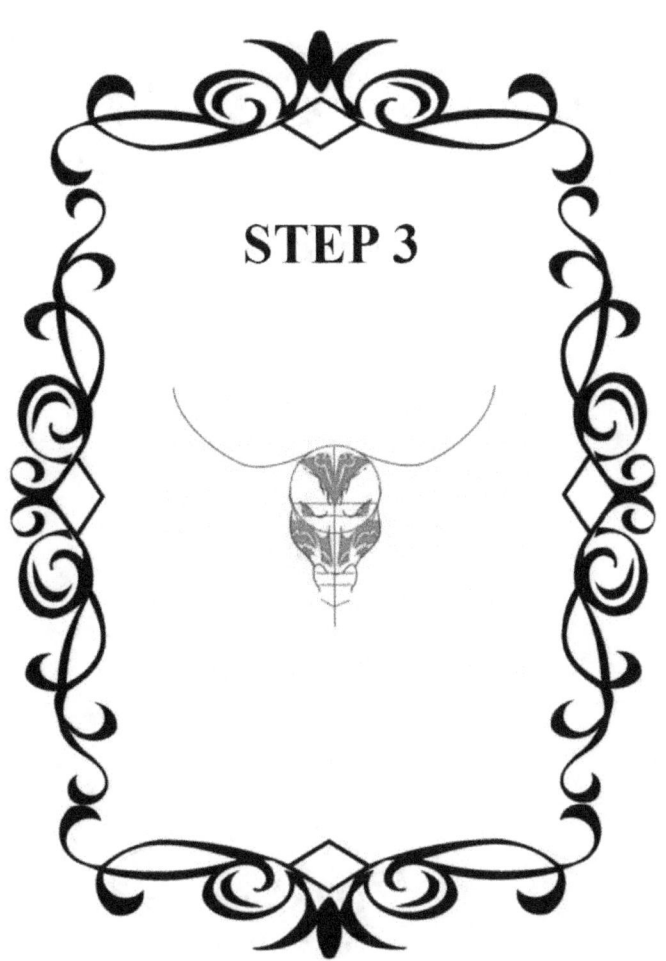

STEP 3

STEP 4

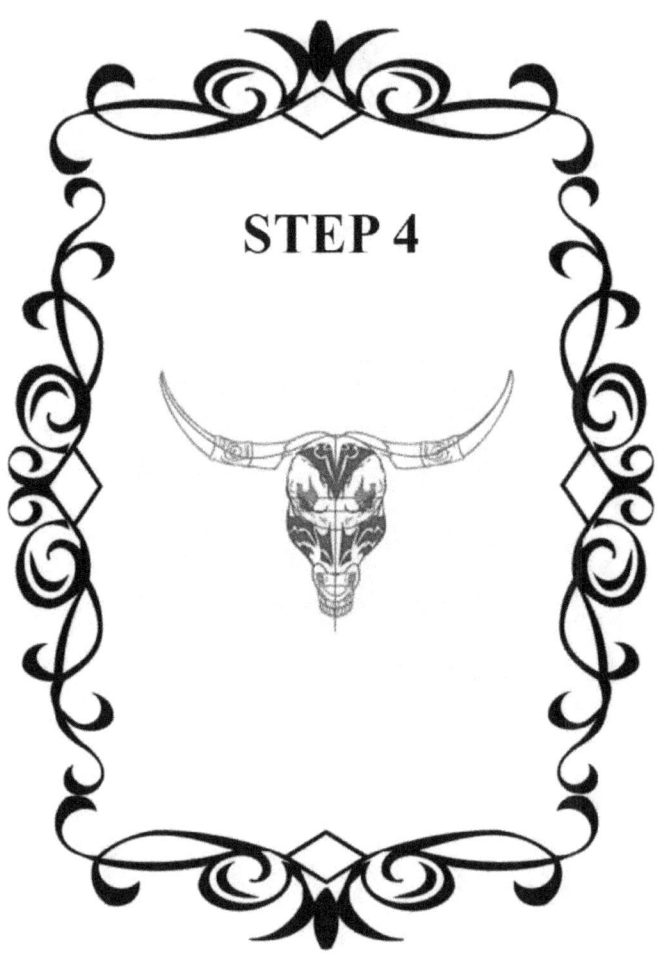

STEP 5

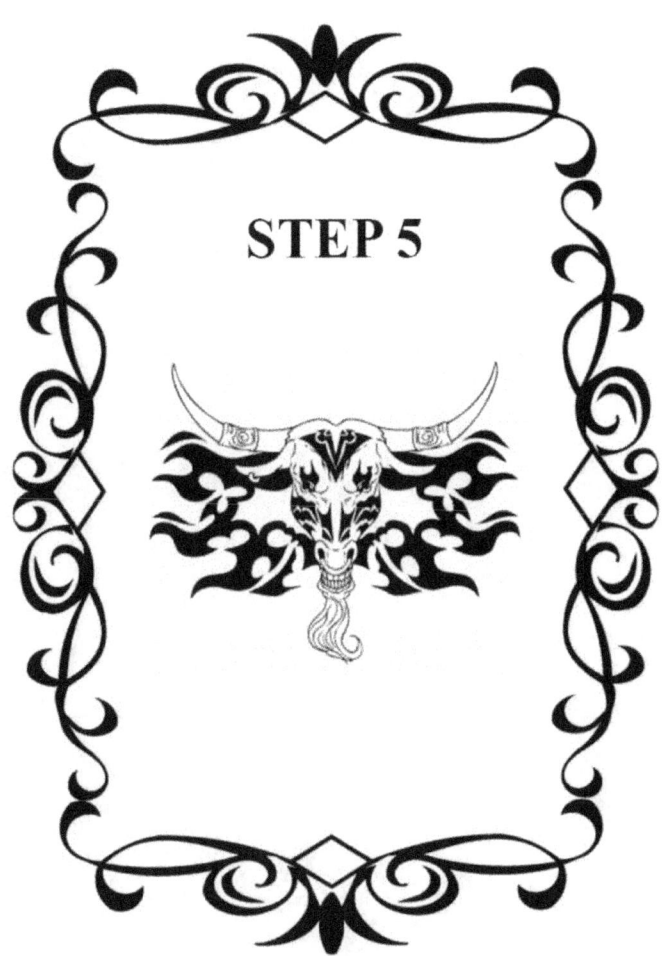

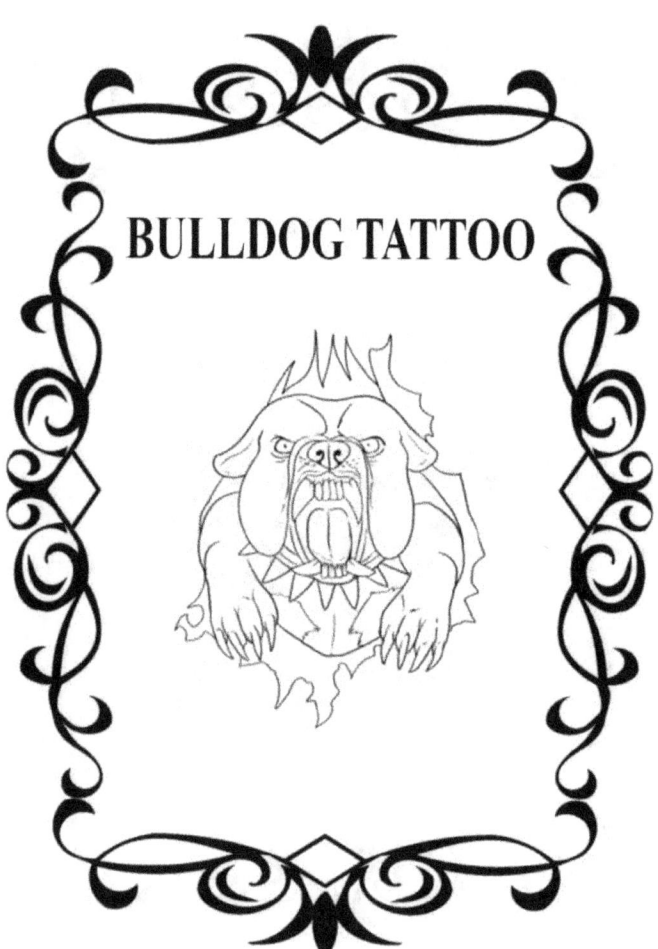

BULLDOG TATTOO

STEP 1

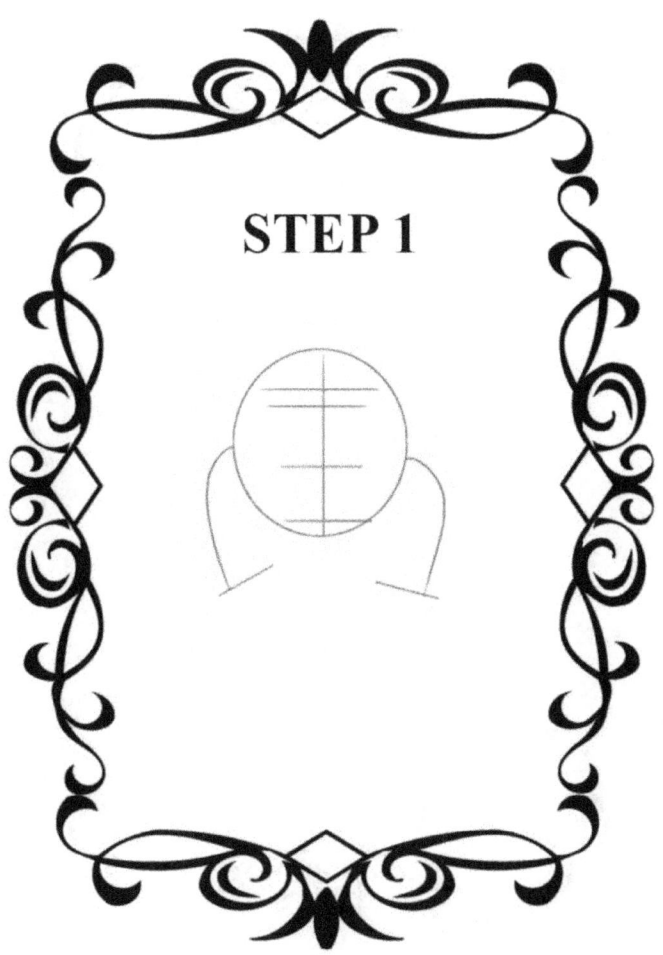

STEP 2

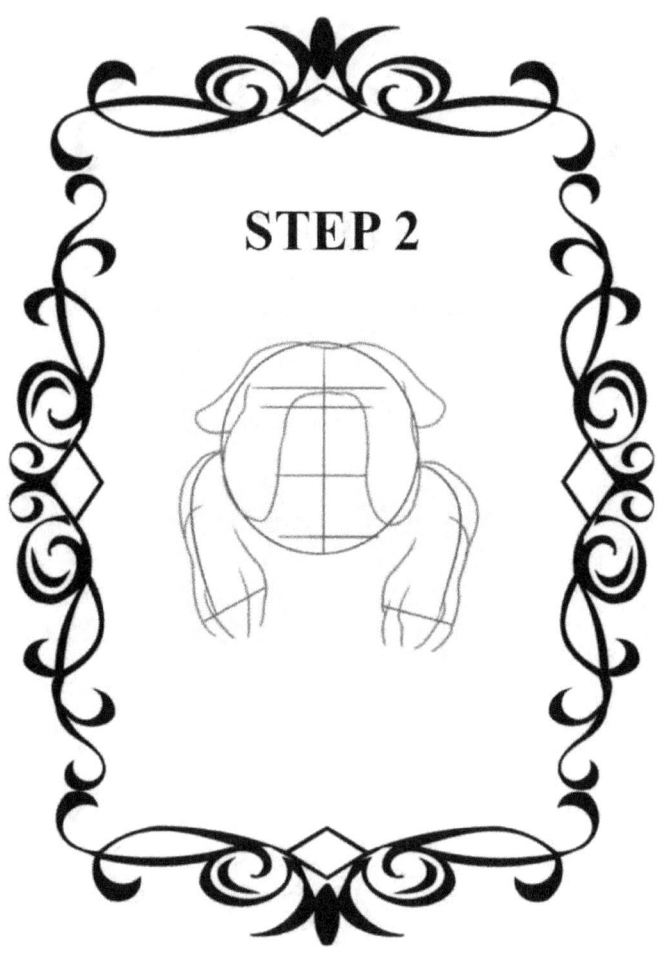

STEP 3

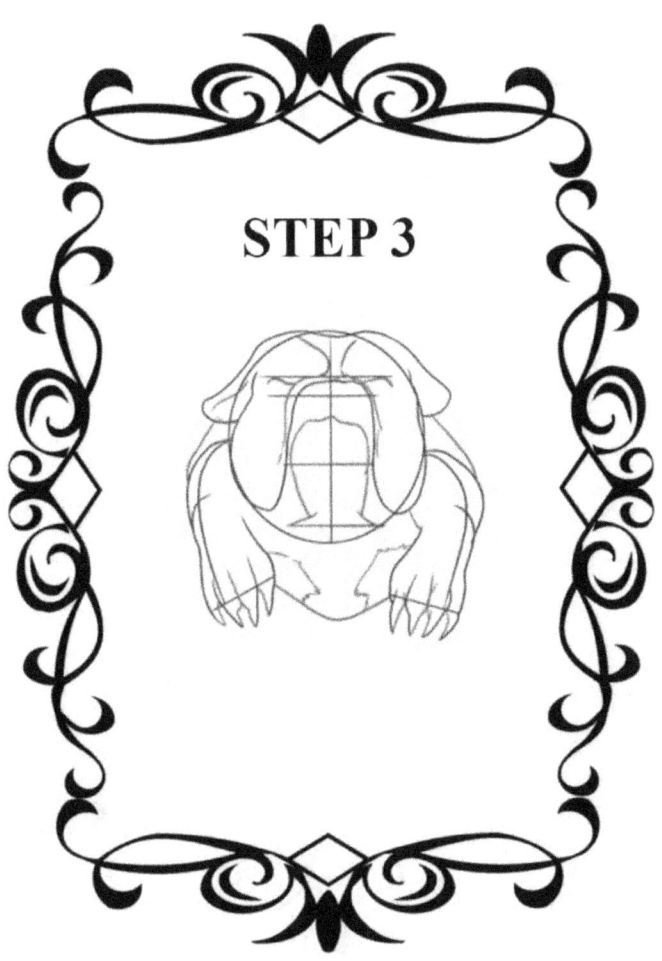

STEP 4

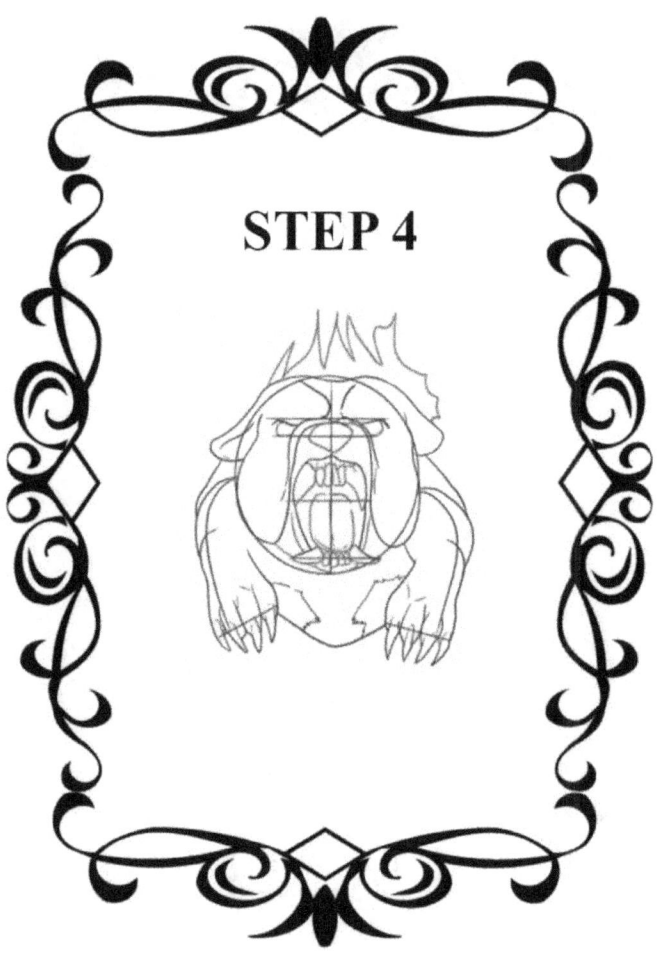

STEP 5

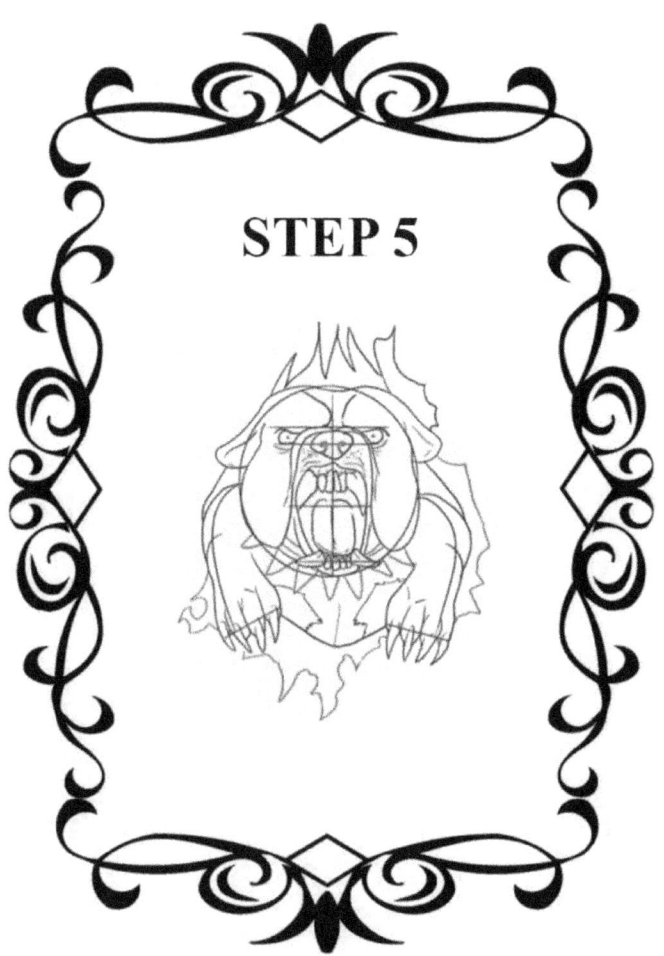

STEP 6

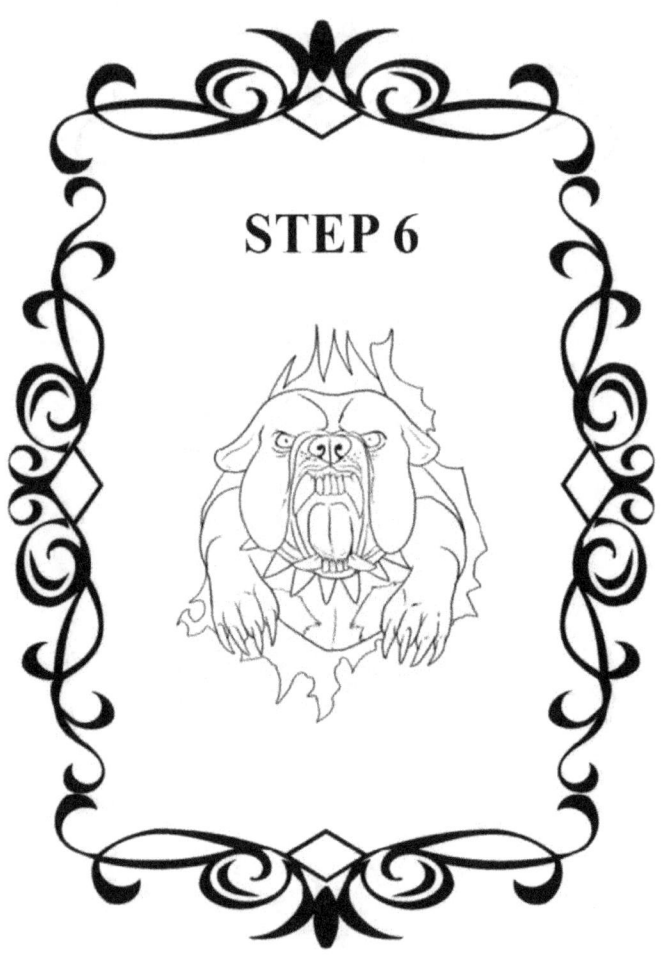

CAT TATTOO

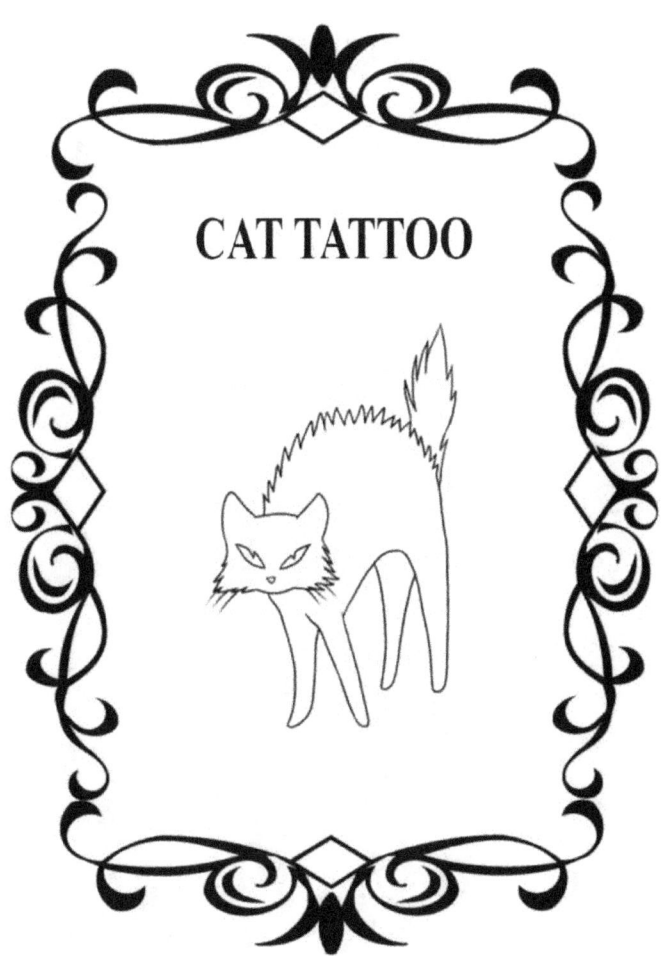

STEP 1

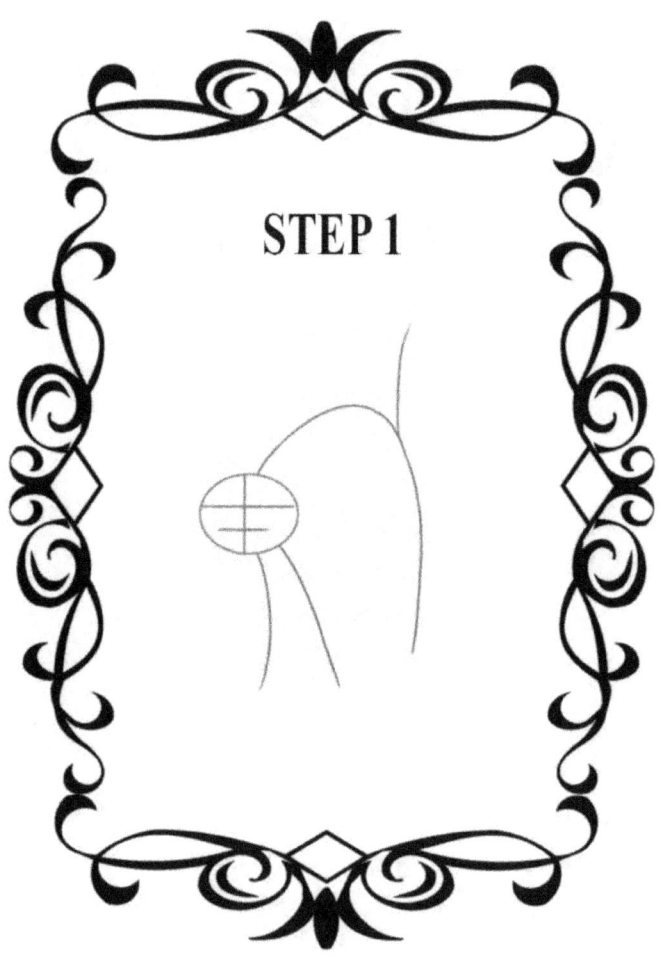

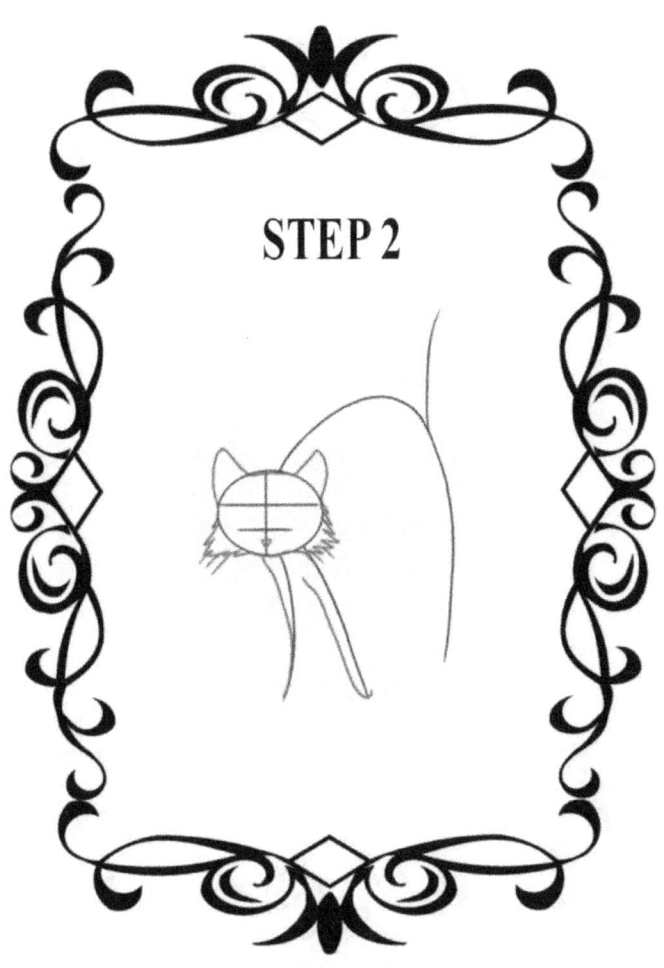

STEP 3

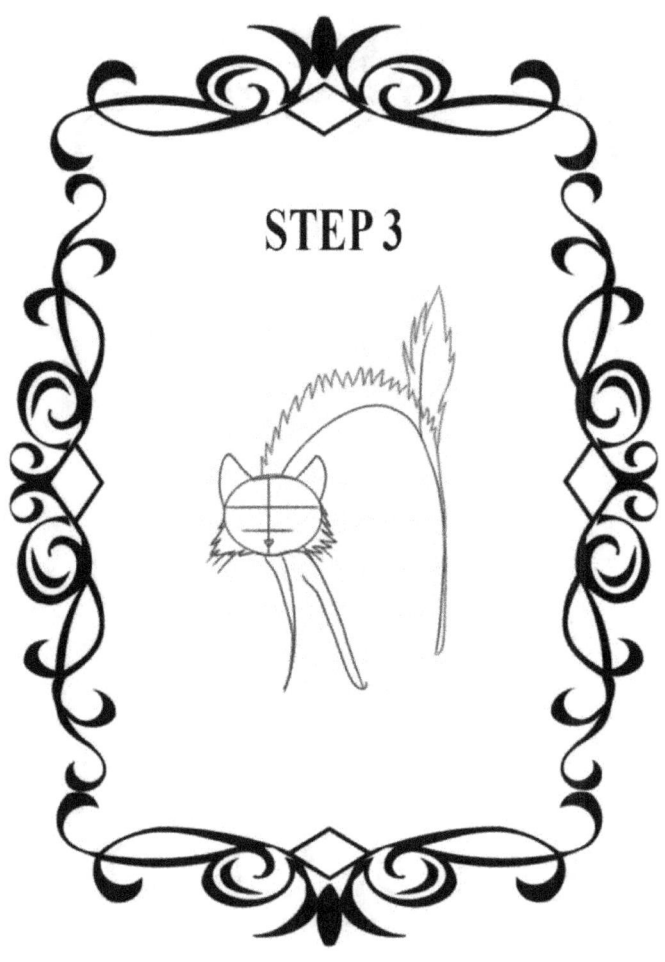

STEP 4

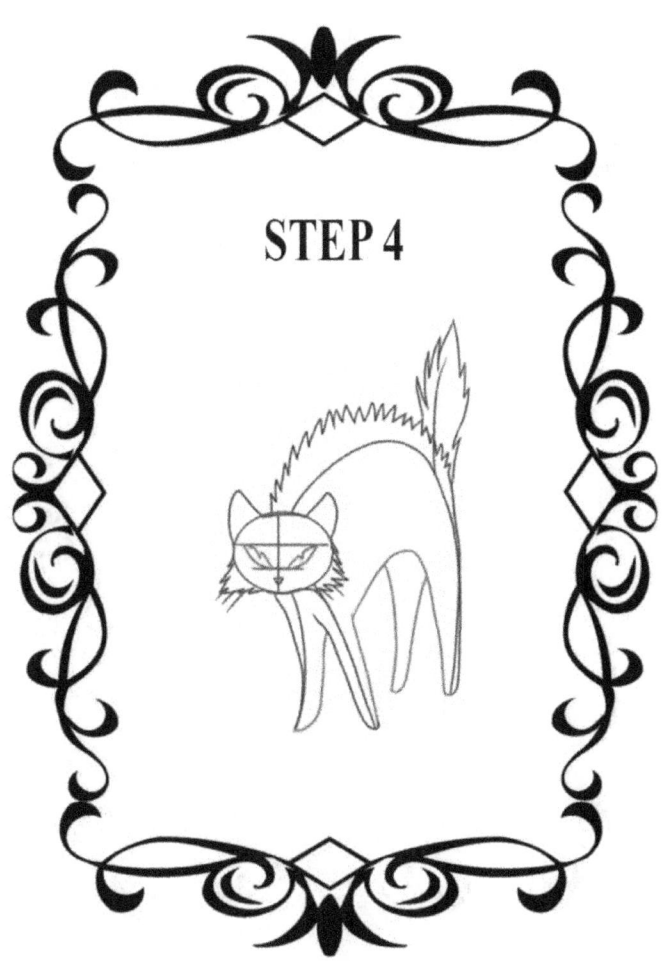

STEP 5

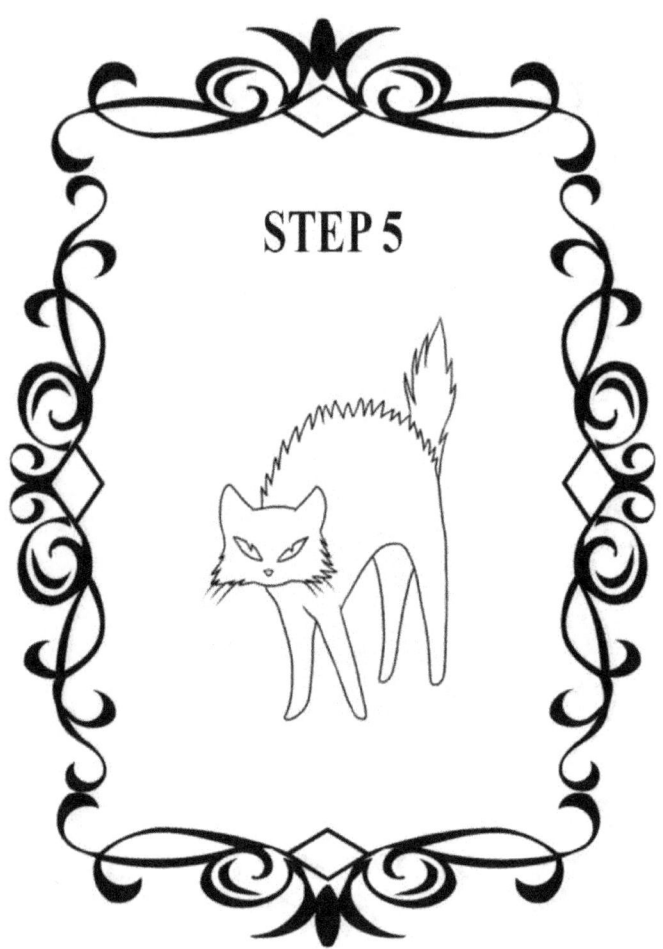

KOI TATTOO

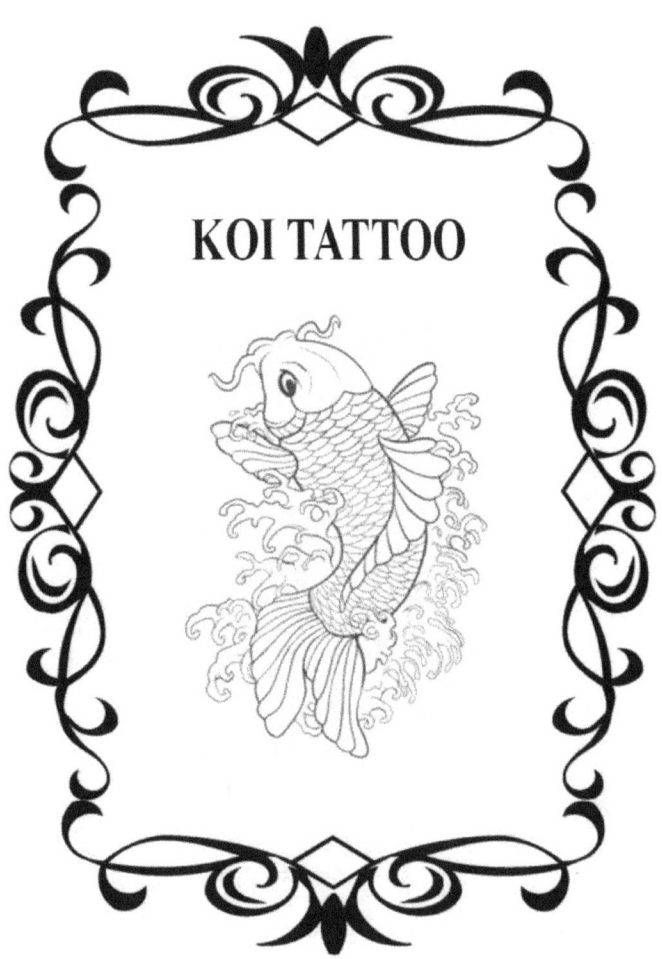

STEP 1

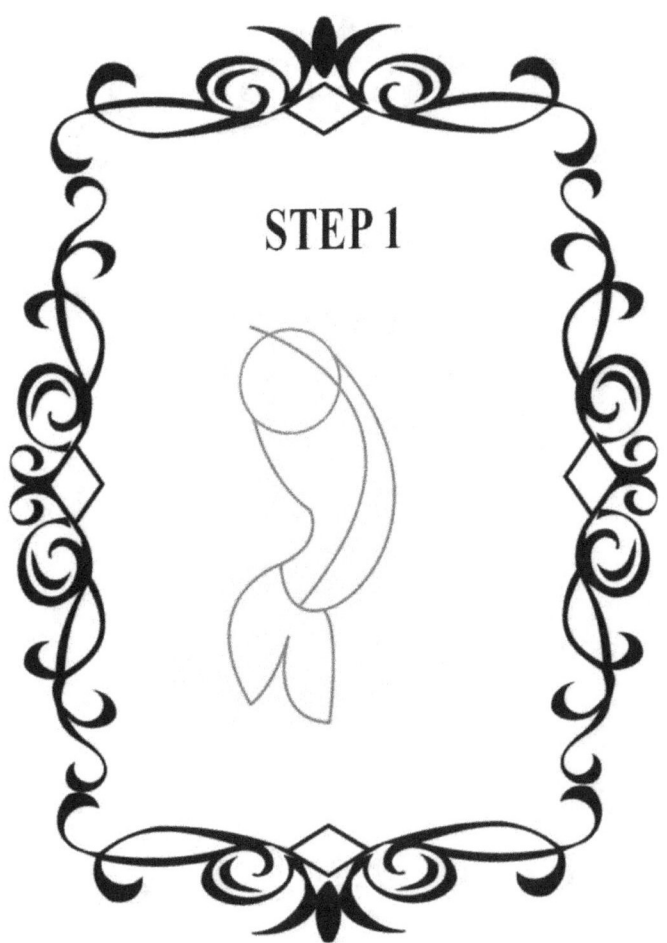

STEP 2

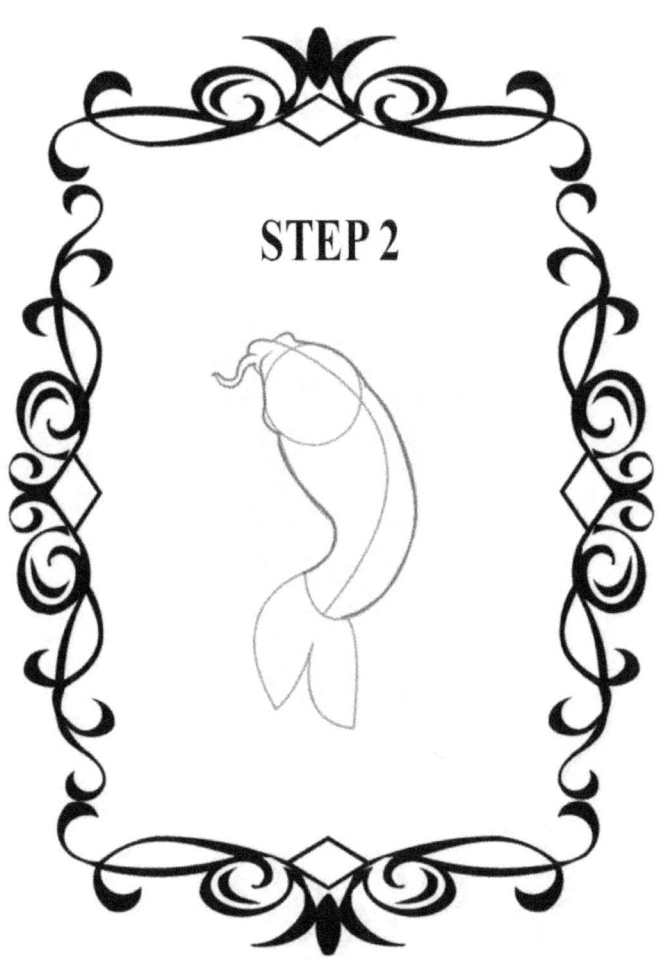

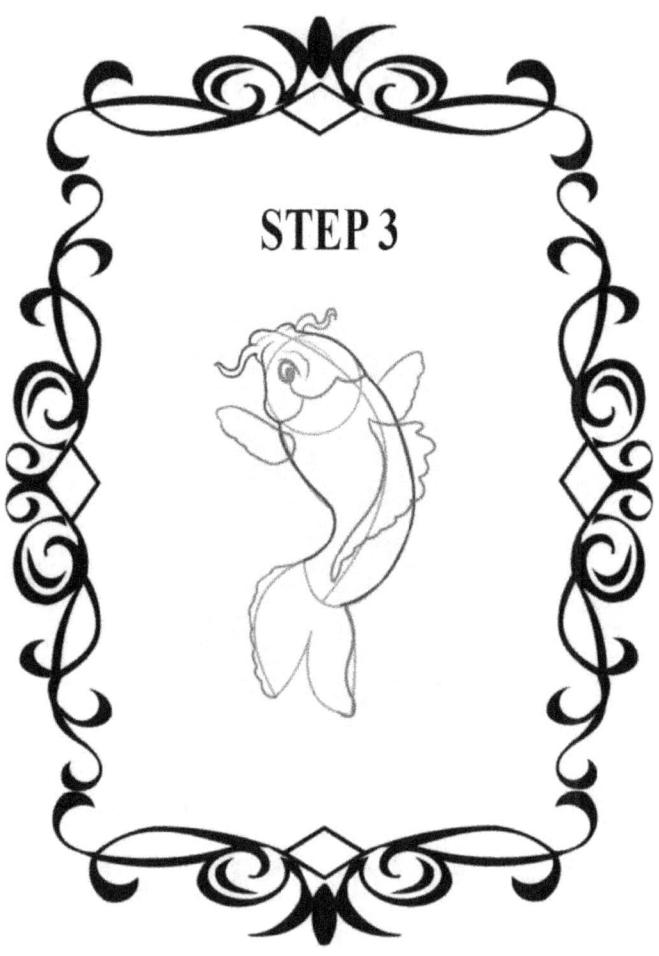

STEP 3

STEP 4

STEP 5

STEP 6

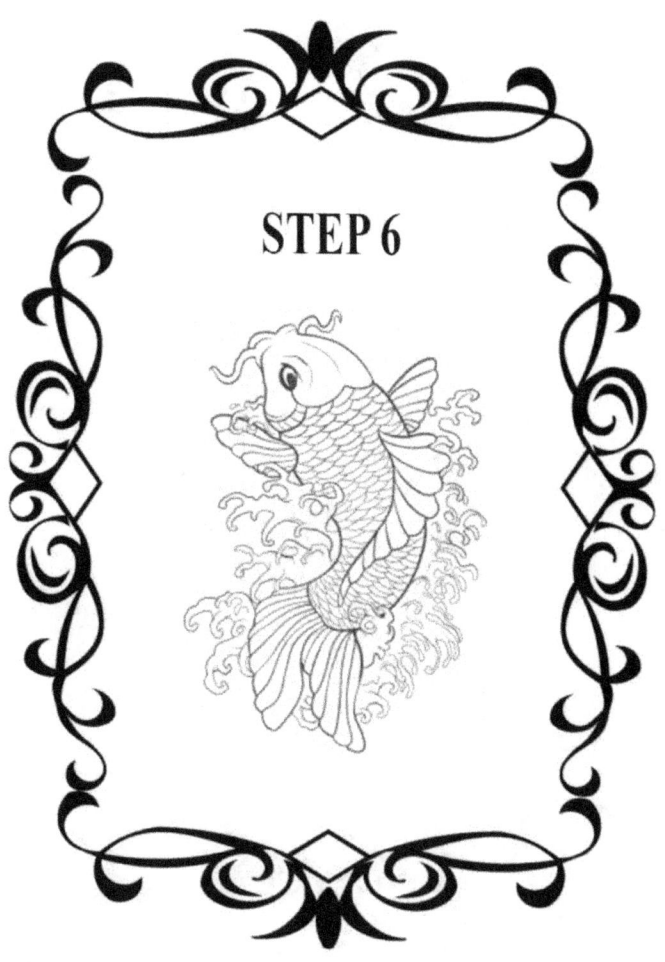

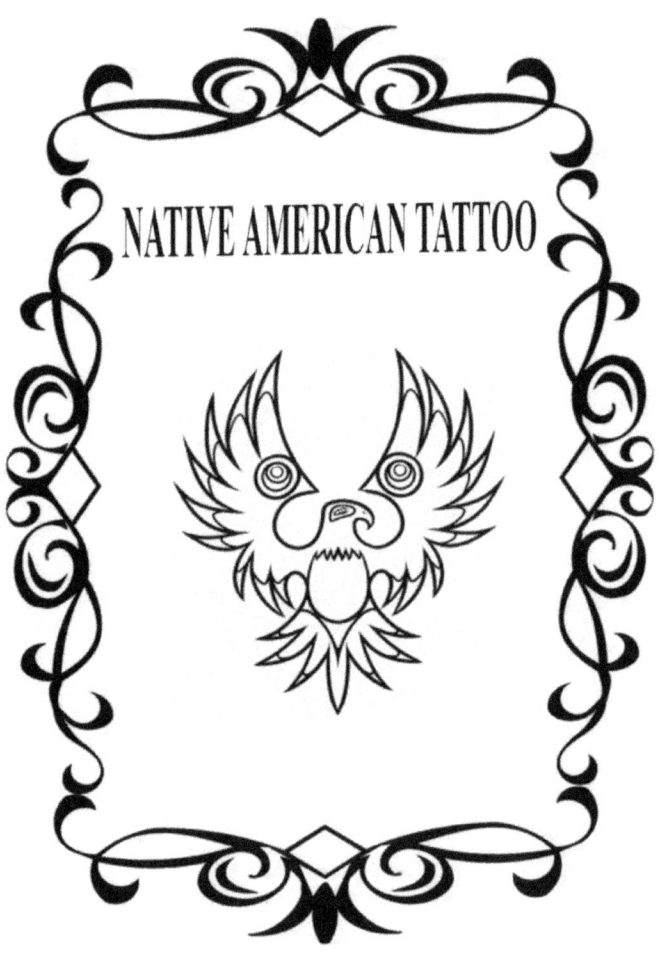

NATIVE AMERICAN TATTOO

STEP 1

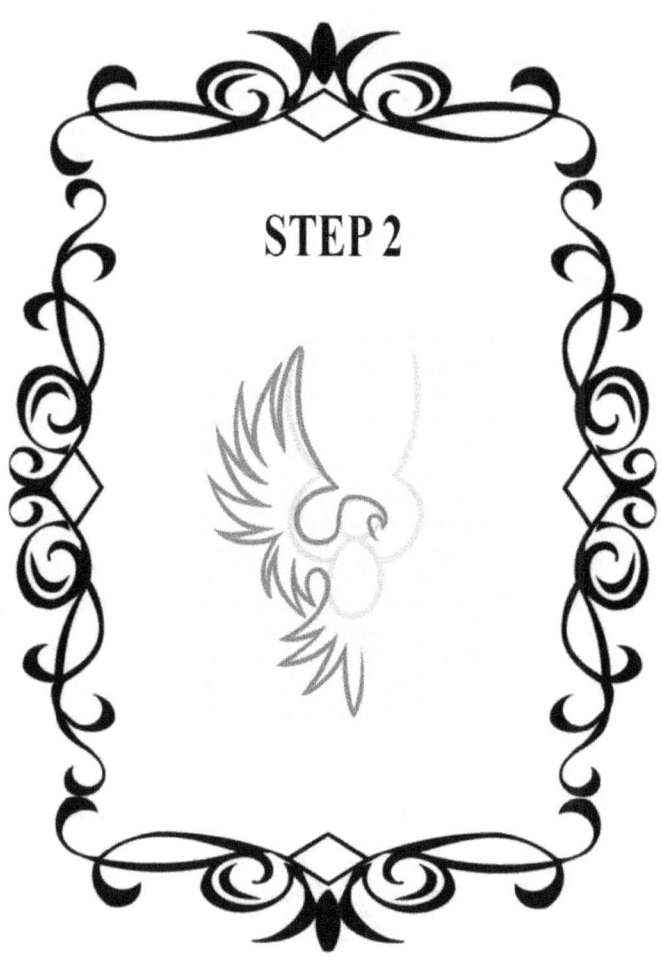

STEP 2

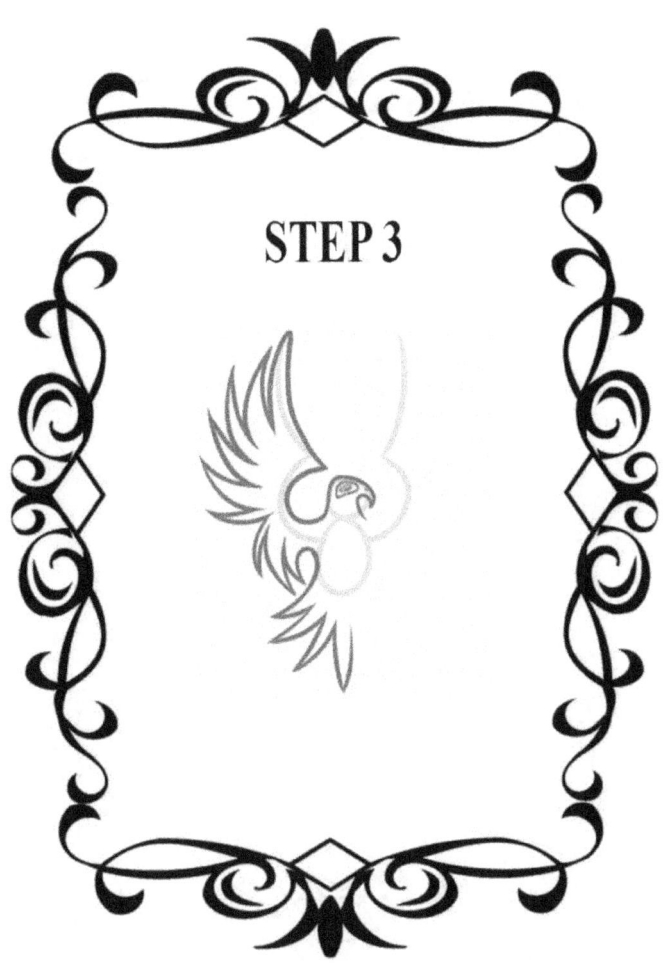

STEP 3

STEP 4

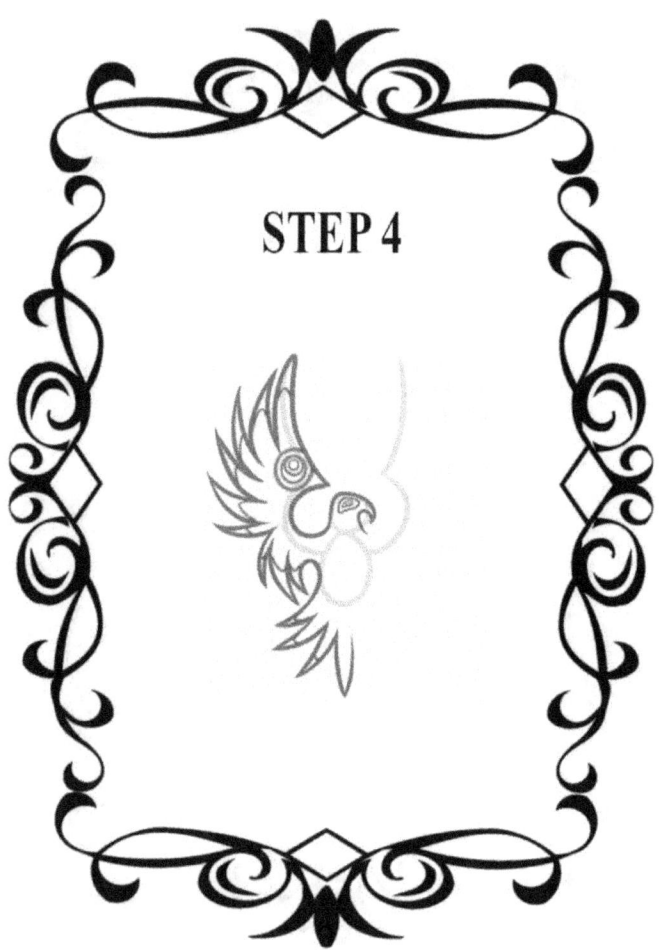

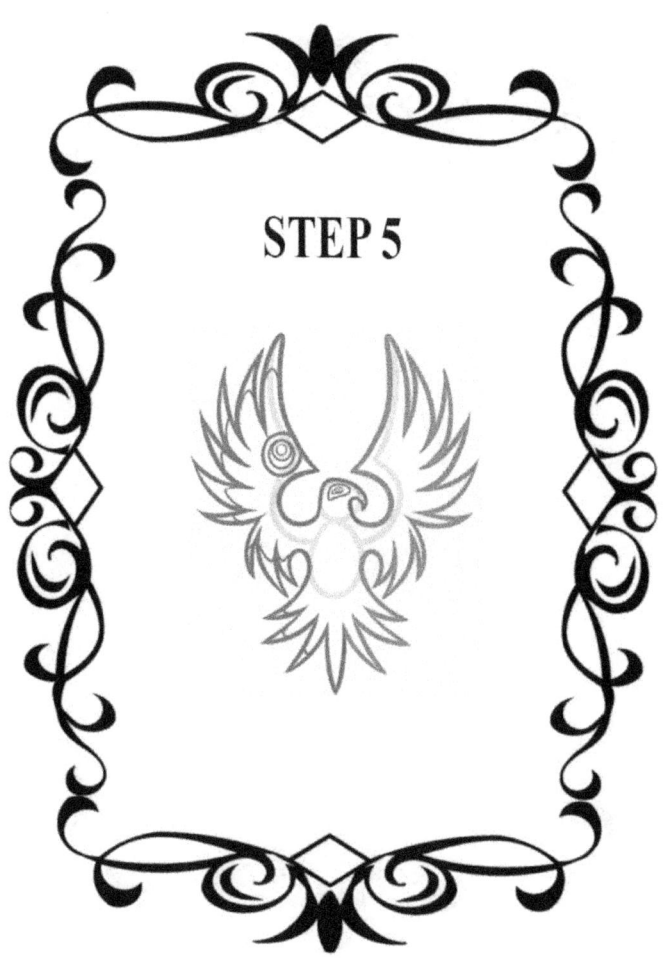

STEP 5

STEP 6

STEP 7

SPIDER TATTOO

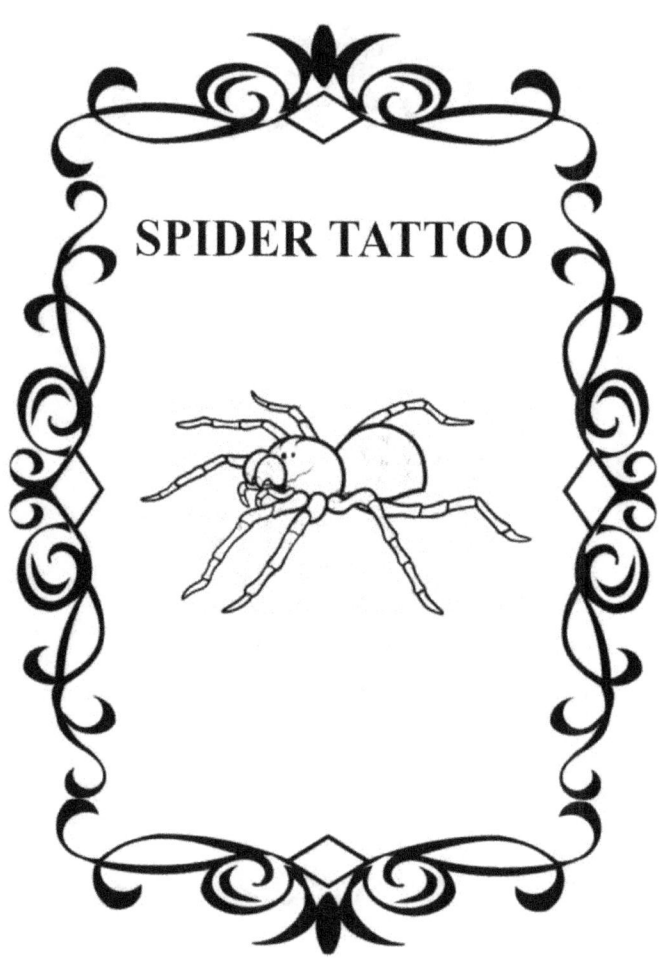

STEP 1

STEP 2

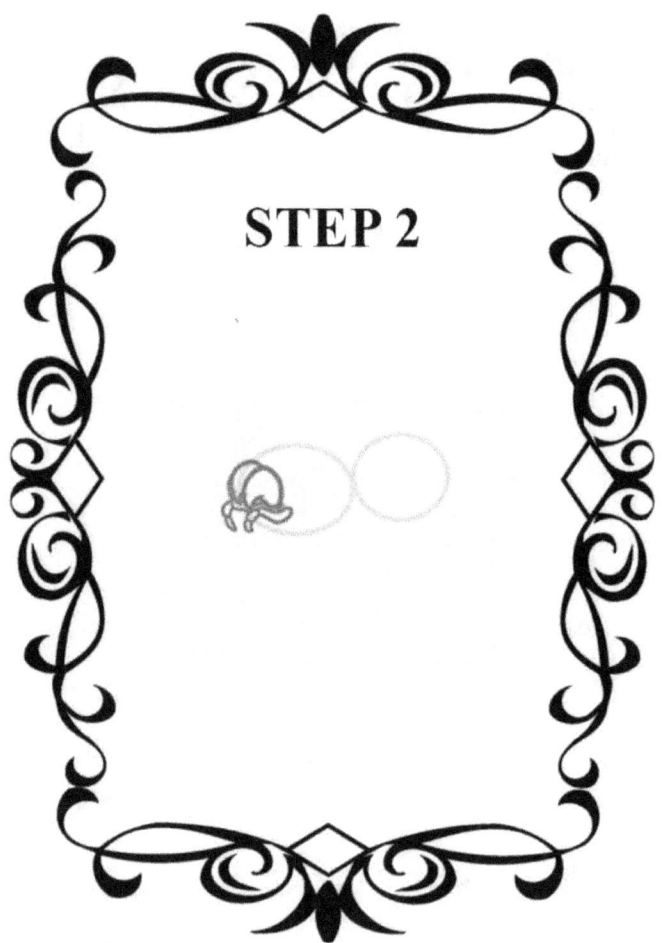

STEP 3

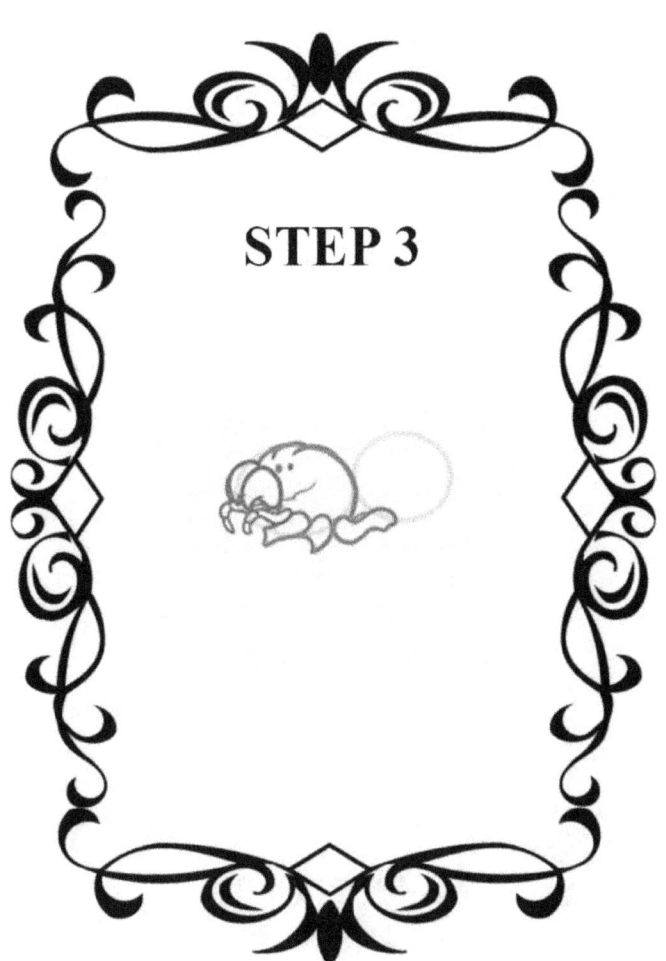

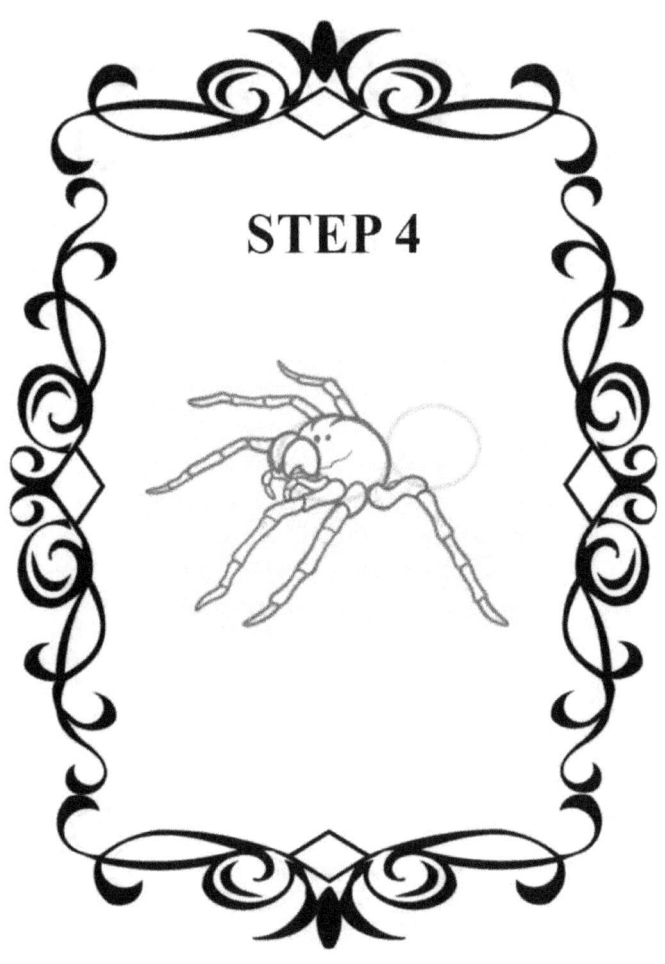

STEP 5

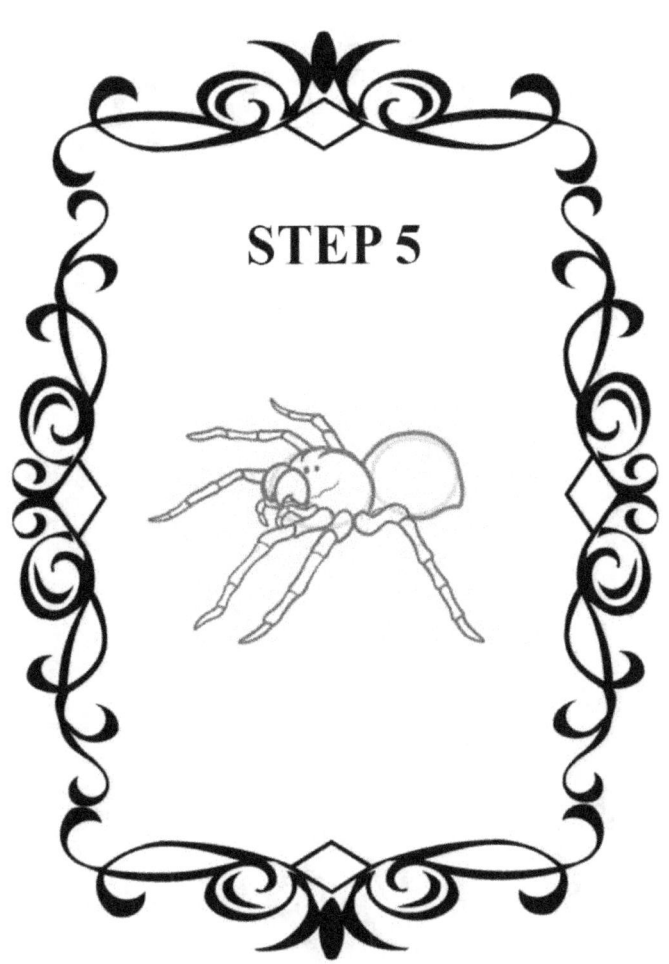

STEP 6

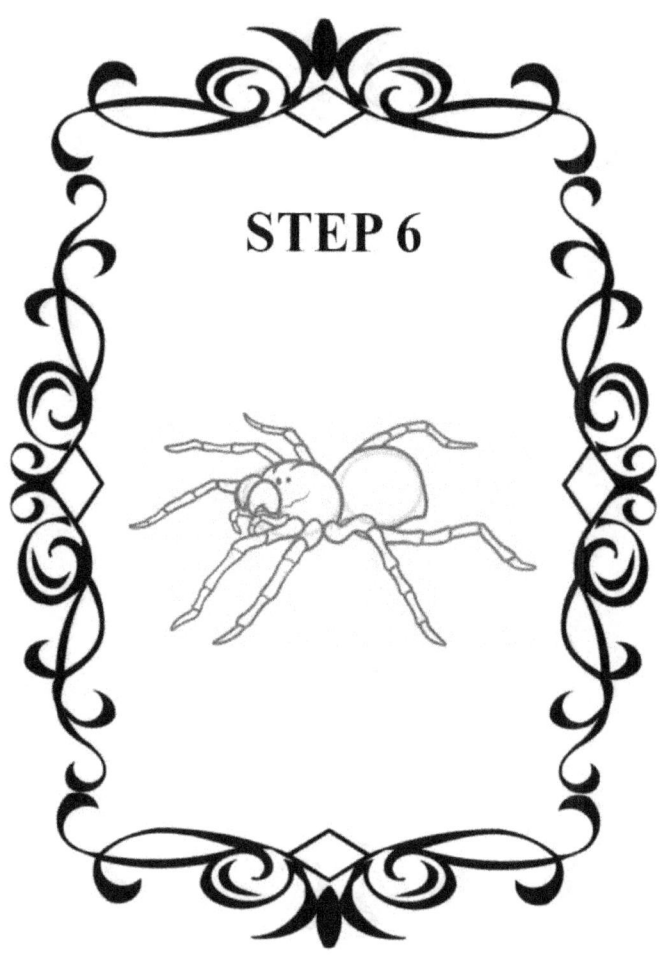

STEP 7

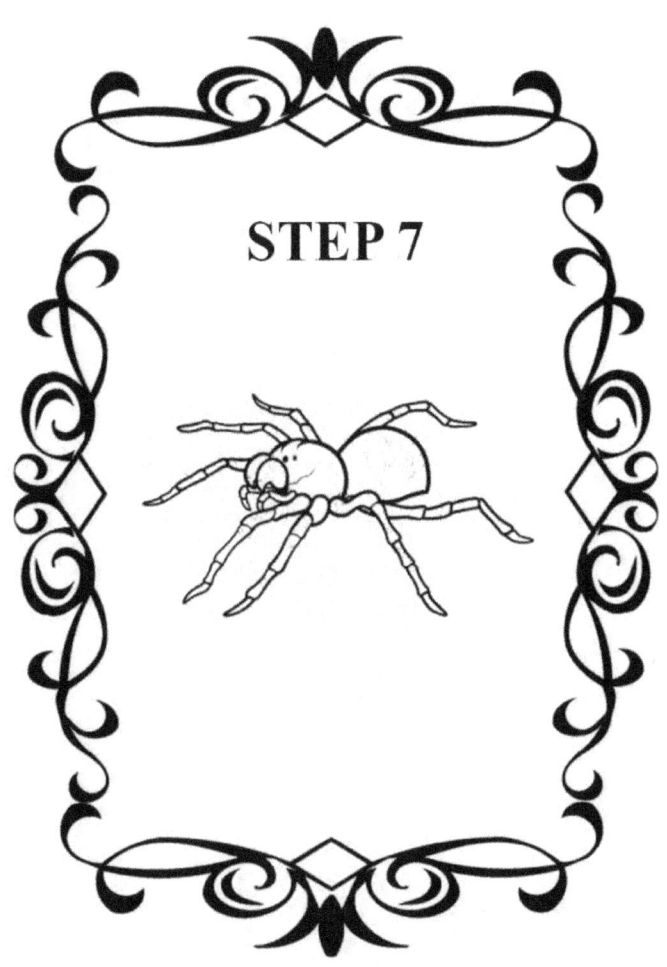

TIGER TATTOO

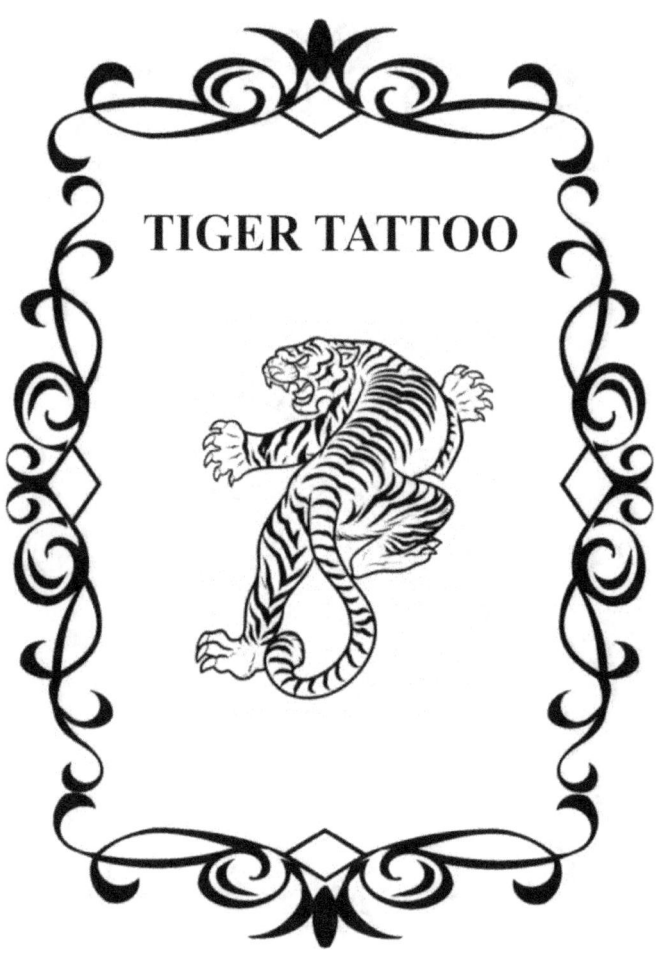

STEP 1

STEP 2

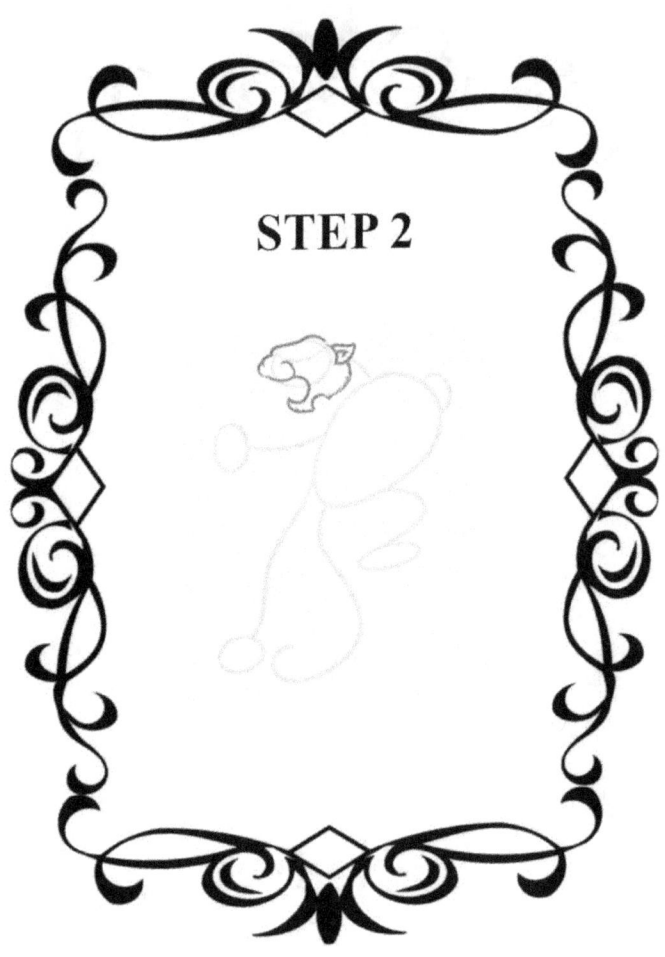

STEP 3

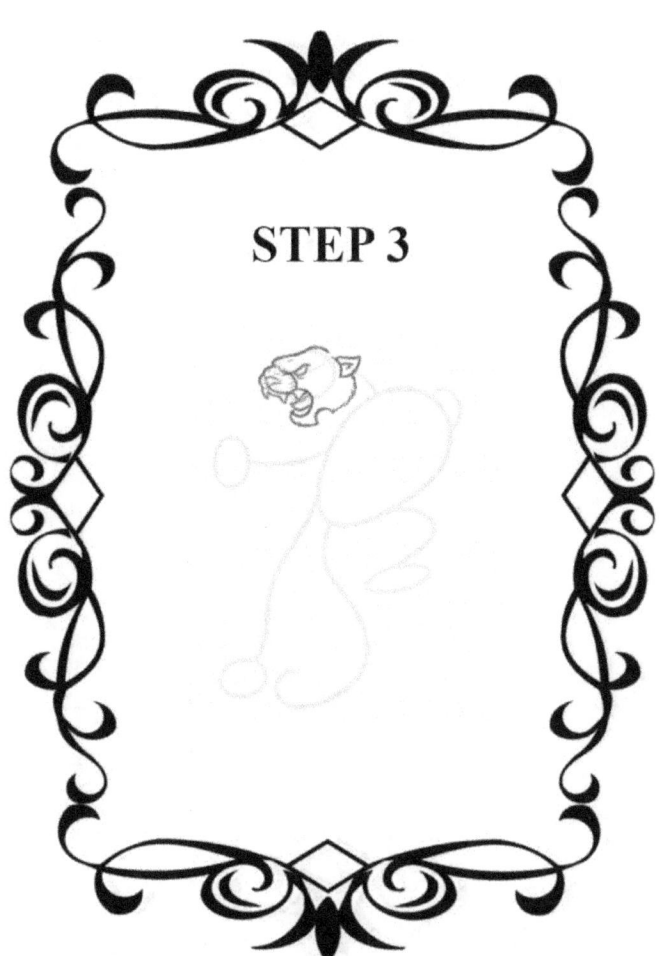

STEP 4

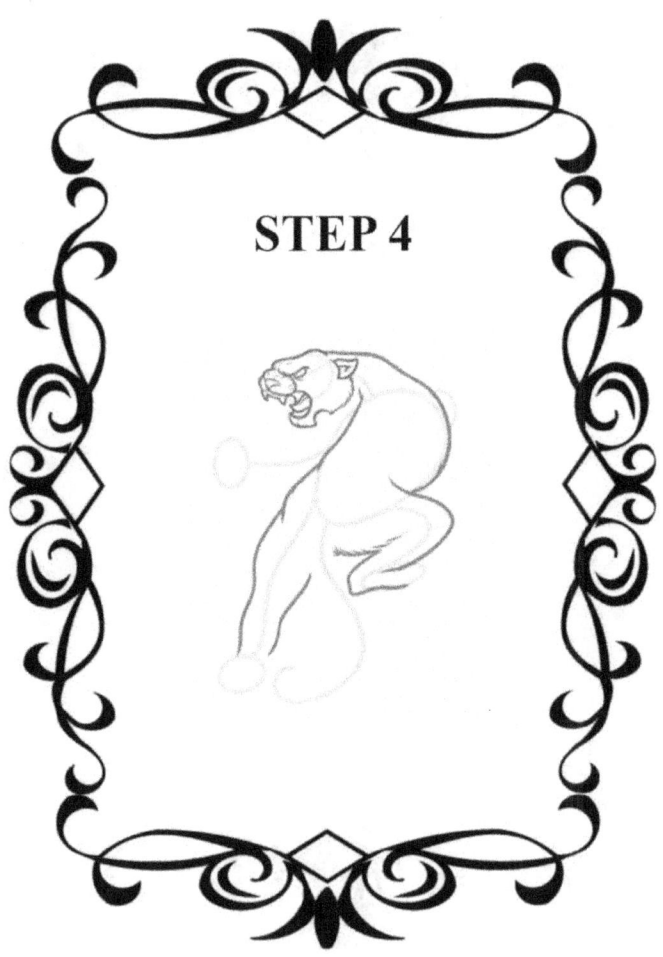

STEP 5

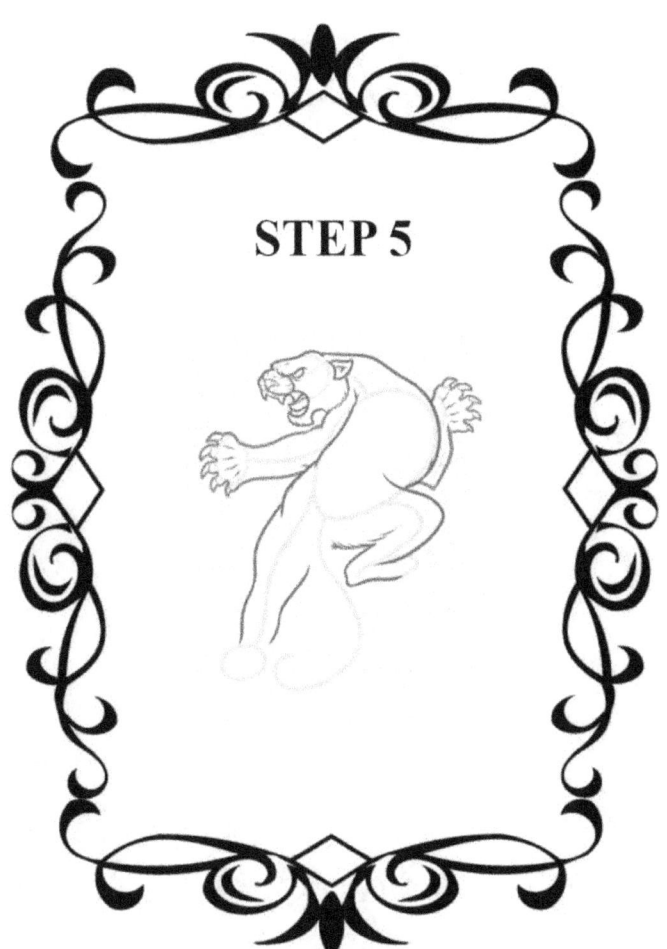

STEP 6

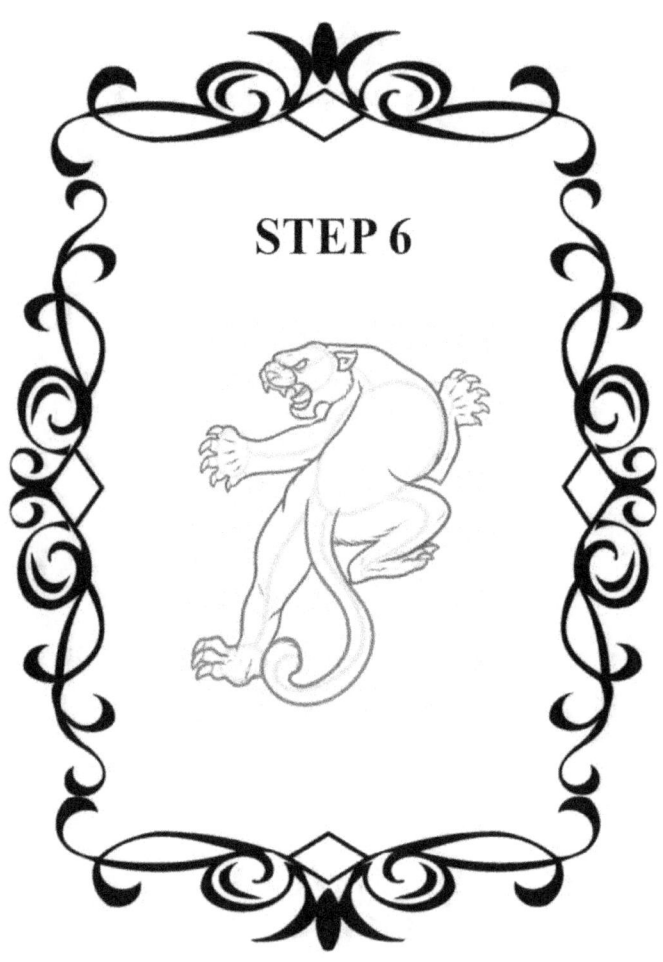

STEP 7

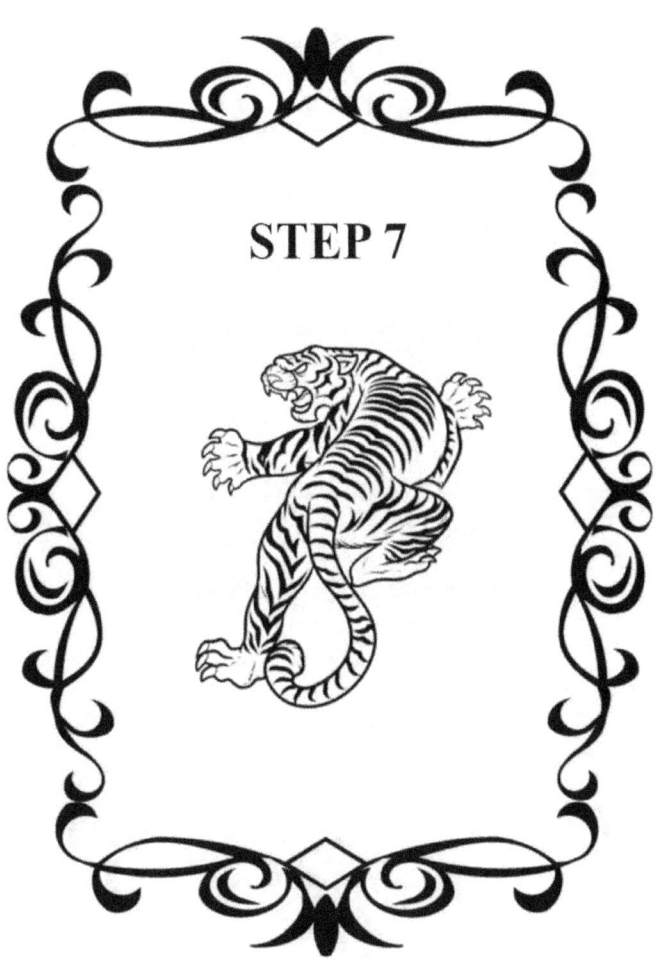

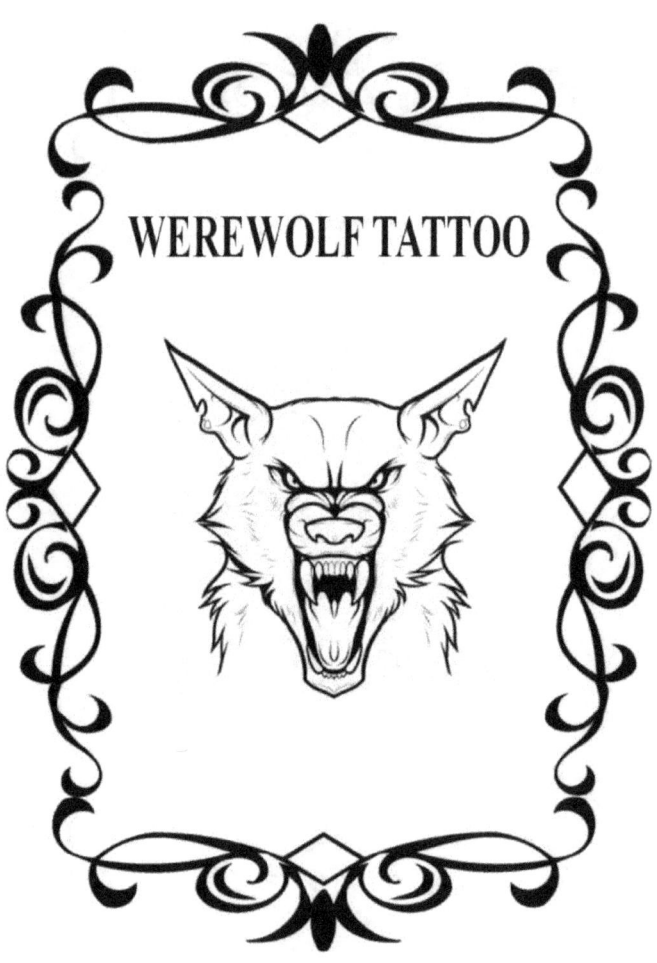

WEREWOLF TATTOO

STEP 2

STEP 3

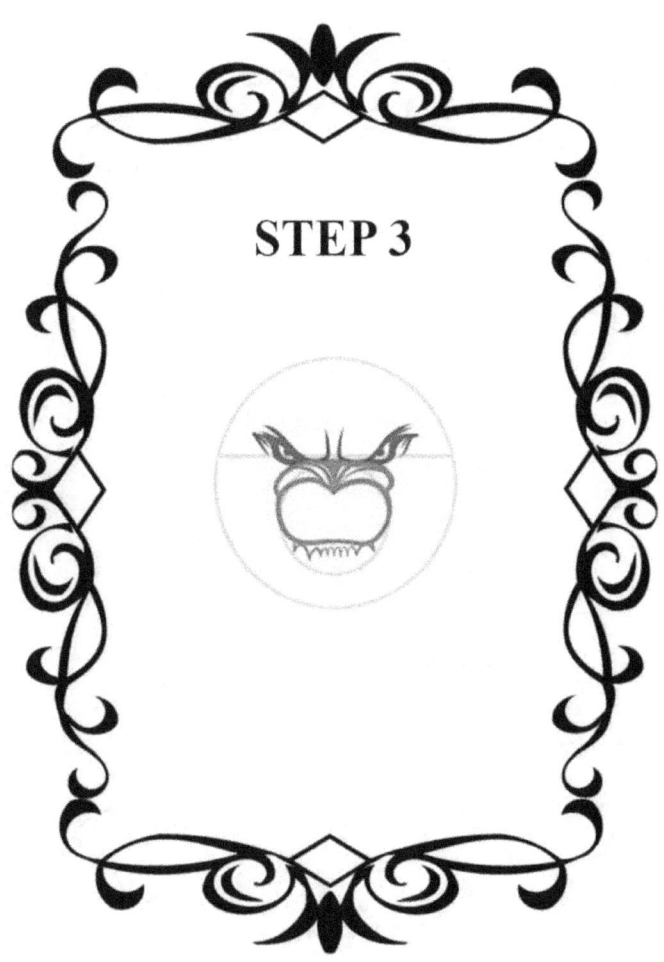

STEP 4

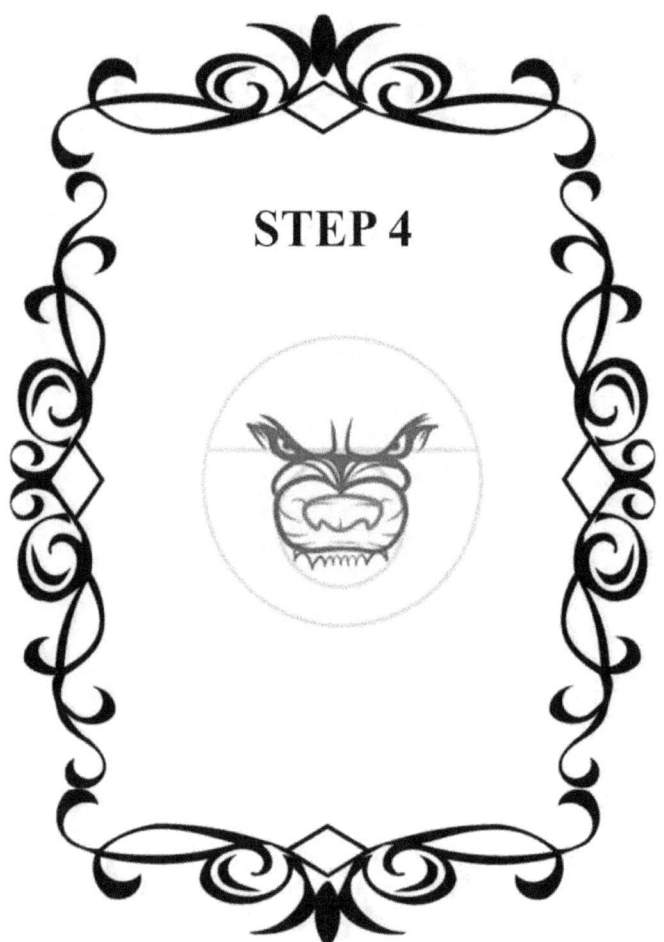

STEP 5

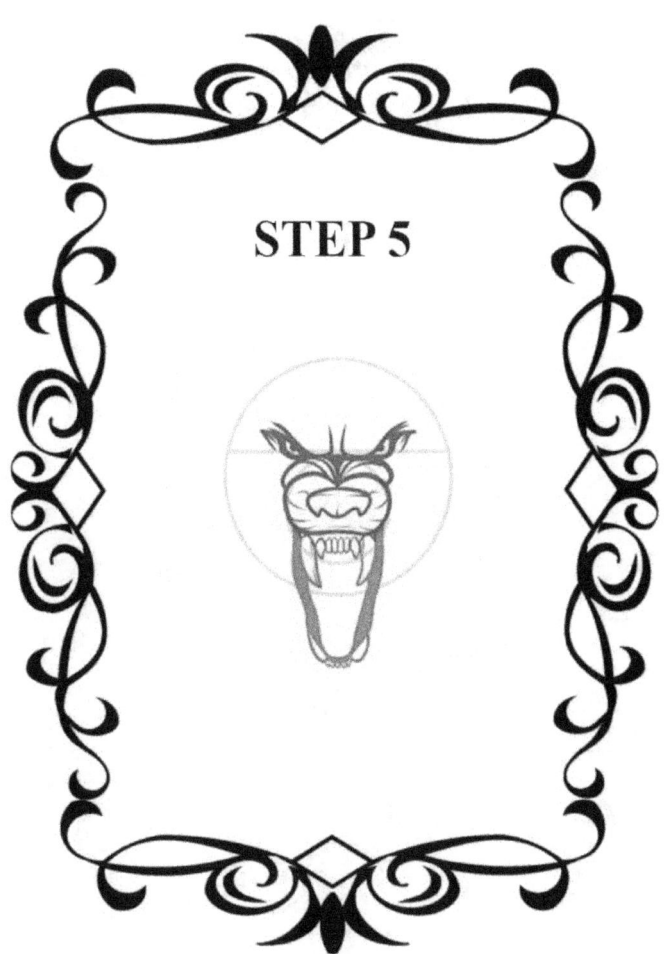

STEP 6

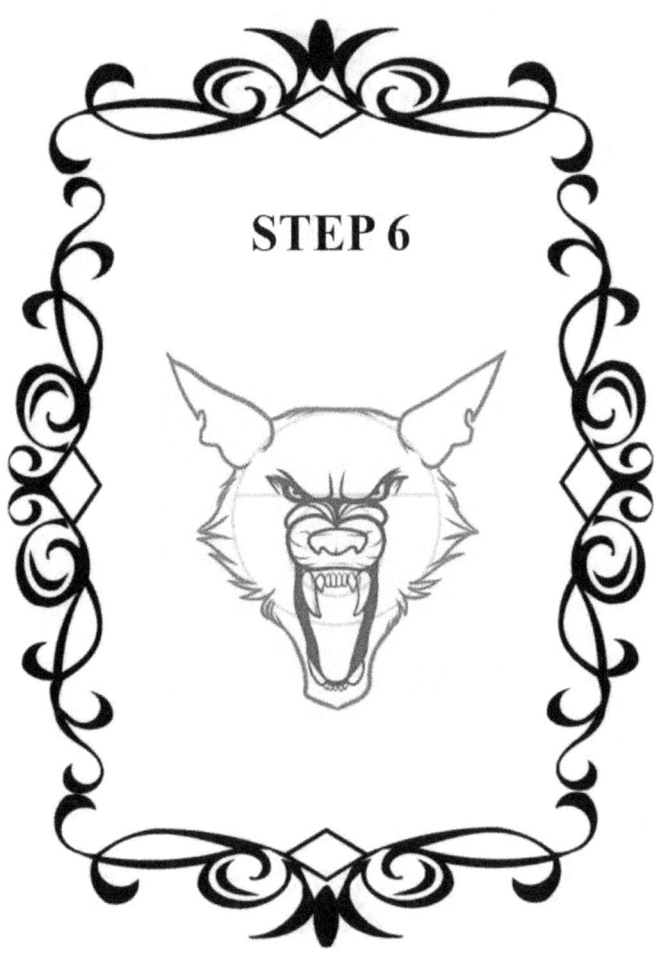

STEP 7

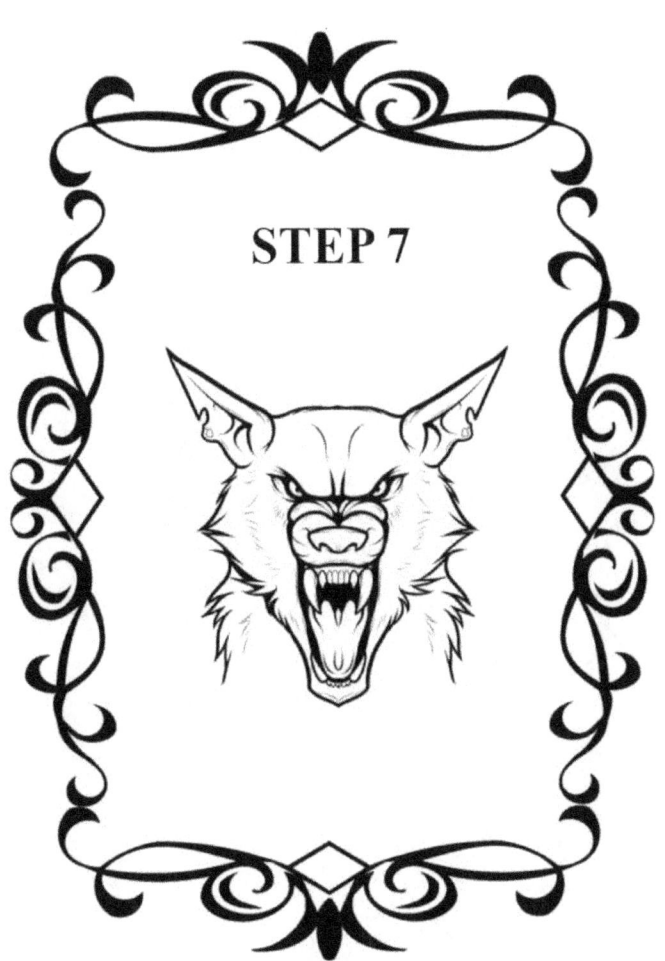

www.ingramcontent.com/pod-product-compliance
Lightning Source LLC
Chambersburg PA
CBHW071616170526
45166CB00003B/1089